REX ELLIS

MOPOKES & MIRAGES

First published 2013

National Library of Australia Cataloguing-in-Publication entry:

Author:	Ellis, Rex, 1942- author.
Title:	Mopokes & mirages / Rex Ellis.
ISBN:	9781922109644 (paperback)
Subjects:	Ellis, Rex, 1942-
	Travelers--Australia--Anecdotes.
	Australia--Description and travel.
	Australia--Social life and customs.
Dewey Number:	919.404

Typeset in Arno Pro 12pt.

Cover Design: Boolarong Press

Front cover: The *Dromedary* on the Darling River by Gary Duncan.

Published by Boolarong Press, Salisbury, Brisbane, Australia.

Printed and bound by Watson Ferguson & Company, Salisbury, Brisbane, Australia.

REX

DEDICATION

To all those who *go the extra mile.* Thank you to:

Front cover design – Garry Duncan

Cartoons – George Aldridge

Maps – The *Map Shop*

Typing – Nicole Hahn

FOREWORD

If Rex Ellis isn't officially a National Treasure, then he should be. And so should Patti Ellis – his wife and partner in every true sense of the word.

Rex has spent his life criss-crossing this wonderful land in every direction, gently but firmly encouraging thousands of others to do the same; persuading them that sleeping under the stars is the only way to go; transporting them hither and yon in a multitude of ways – four-wheel drive, Shanks's pony, truck, camel, raft, tinny, paddle-wheeler, rubber-ducky; showing them the beauty of desert, rain-forest, mountain, island, river and lake – including his beloved Lake Eyre. From south to north and back, from east to west – and not forgetting that gem of the south, Tasmania.

Patti has been there with him on many of these amazing explorations, sharing the load and starring with the camp-fire cooking. And the rest of the time she's been keeping the home fires burning – and the whole organisation running smoothly.

Here are just a few of my own many treasured memories:

Gliding across the khaki-coloured flood-waters of the Cooper in a rosy dawn, after an hilarious night spent in the boats…

Sitting alone in a rock gallery up the Prince Regent river, watching a pair of rainbow bee-eaters for ages…

Waking up one morning by the Coongie Lakes to fine a spoonbill calmly fishing about a metre away from my swag…

Hearing Rex playing "Waltzing Matilda" on his mouth-organ round the campfire, while his ever-present Jack Russell sang along…

Well, you can see what I mean, can't you? Along with many others, I thank Rex and Patti for these and many other wonderful experiences and memories.

Eileen Nelson

A grateful traveller with Rex for more than forty years!

INTRODUCTION

Any ornithologist understands about Mopokes, but I had better spell it out for the non-ornithologists. At night, you may hear that evocative Australian *mopoke* sounding call. Next day you will often flush a longish mottled grey bird with startling yellow and black eyes. Or the more observant of you will spy it sitting on a horizontal branch, its excellent camouflage seeming to make it part of the tree itself. But it's a great hoax. The bird you heard at night is the little brown Boobook owl, *(boobook, mopoke,* similar sounding calls) rarely seen in daylight, and what most of the population thinks is the *mopoke* is actually a Tawny Frogmouth. It's a great pity, but there's no such bird as a Mopoke, which is a sad waste of a great sounding name.

This book is my usual mix of Outback *stuff*. I keep trying to highlight the positive and negatives of our great country. Free speech still allows you to have a go at the ever increasing bureaucracy that is slowly stifling the Aussie way of life, and this right must be preserved at all costs. I have had some great mates (and still have) and without them would not have been able to run my business or pursue the lifestyle I have. A few of these are mentioned here, some dead and some alive. From the two legged, four legged (camels/dogs) to the four wheel drives that have been the mainstay of my business. A word or two on them.

How I met and married my greatest mate of all, gets a run, plus plenty more.

No one has an excuse for not reading my books, because each chapter is like a small book. Any one (even *non-readers*) can read a chapter before they go to bed, so keep that in mind. I need the sales!

Running my Outback Safari business has given me the privilege of meeting and travelling with lots of wonderful people, who have not only contributed to my livelihood, but many have become lifelong friends.

We have to keep having *fun* — harder all the time as the *nanny state* encroaches on our daily lives. The Aussie Larrikin spirit must be kept alive.

Rex Ellis

CONTENTS

1
ACQUIRING THE BIRDSVILLE PUB

On a crisp clear morning in late October 1972, Patti and I walked into the bar of the Birdsville Pub. The only other occupant was the publican, Len Gaffrey, behind the bar, tidying up.

We had spent the night there with our party, returning south from our annual Cape York Peninsula Safari. I had my cheque book with me to pay for the accommodation, which I did. Len took the cheque and placed it in the till. After chatting for a couple of minutes, there was a pause before Len looked at us and said "Rex and Patti, I think you ought to buy this old Pub". I stared back at Len, realizing that he was fair dinkum about this, and thankful that I had just consumed a solid breakfast.

My reply was something like "Len, thanks for the thought, but we are not Publicans, and we couldn't afford it anyway". Len disagreed, and when he named a price, I had to take it very seriously! I had a very strong feeling that this was one opportunity I needed to 'yard up'. With this in mind I suggested that Patti and I ought to have a walk up Adelaide Street (the main drag) to consider this.

We did that, and by the time we arrived back at the pub, we had decided to buy it. Didn't have the money, but it was 'gettable'. So, it was with a feeling of suppressed excitement that we walked back into the bar and told Len he had a deal. You wouldn't describe him as an emotional type of person, but he broke into a wide smile, and we shook hands on it. The fact that Len was a teetotaler and we were about to head down the Birdsville track with a party of people, were good enough reasons not to have a drink on it – as well as being just after breakfast!

There was a busy time ahead of us. After one of our most successful safari seasons ever, Patti and I had made plans to go to Europe and Africa (see 'Ten Thousand Campfires') leaving in November and not returning to Australia until February the following year. We had made arrangements with Len to take the pub over in early March 1973, on our return.

One thing uppermost in our minds was that of finding a suitable couple to manage the pub, as Patti and I would keep operating our safari business. This was still on our minds as we flew to the U.K., and it was on this flight that the idea came to me. As far as I was concerned, a bush pub required a bush publican. I was well aware that a publican can make or break a pub.

For a number of years I had known a dog fence netting rider who lived with his wife and kids at Toona Gate on the NSW/Queensland border where the Dingo Proof Fence is just that. I used to call in to the hut where they lived, on my safaris in the area. The Toona Gate in the dog fence is on a route I used to take north-west of Tibooburra, when travelling between Broken Hill and Innamincka.

Taffy's wife Silvia and their four young kids were very much a bush family. Taffy, a Welshman and seaman, who jumped his ship in Australia as a young man was a bushman in the true sense of the word, who happened to possess what was probably the largest collection of Aboriginal artefacts outside of museums in Australia. Silvia (Silvie) was a strong confident bush woman. They lived a sparten existence, but were very much a happy and capable family.

I had sent a telegram to Taffy as soon as we landed in London, offering him the job, and saying that I would phone him in Tibooburra in a couple of nights time. I duly phoned him from our hotel room on a cold, rainy night, and at the end of the conversation, he had agreed enthusiastically to take on the job. He would resign his job on the dog fence and move his family to Birdsville. It was arranged that I would accompany them to Birdsville soon after arriving home from Africa in early March.

So it was that in March 1973 the Nicholl's family and myself, left Adelaide in my new Range Rover and Taffy's much loved Ford Fairlane, both vehicles loaded to the hilt with mostly Nicholls' belongings. Taffy had organised for the rest of the gear, including his artefact collection to be brought up from Tibooburra at a later date.

I was a bit concerned, particularly regarding Taffy's vehicle, as a few days earlier there had been big rains on the Birdsville Track, the heaviest falls on the top end of the track. We had a good run to Marree, and although the track was wet and fairly slow, I only had to give Taffy a tow through one wet patch. However, on the other side of Clifton Hills Station it was a very different story. After the Fairlane being bogged several times, I decided to keep it permanently on the tow rope. After that, apart from permanently hanging off the back of me, the Fairlane wasn't the problem. The Range Rover was. There are good things about Range Rovers, but plenty of bad things as well, particularly in those early ones. The worst, in my opinion, was the electric fuel pump located at the fuel tank, where it would get drenched whenever we went through water with any depth, which on this occasion was almost all the time. To cut a long story shorter, it took us two days to get from Clifton Hills to the Diamantina River flood plain, south of Birdsville, all a bit the worse for wear, although the kids were in high spirits looking on the episode as a great adventure.

Duc to big monsoonal rains in the catchment, the Diamantina was in flood and Birdsville cut off by road. Lorry Morton at Pandie Station contacted Birsdville by radio, and the next day 'Blue Mouldy Bill' (the handyman who went with the pub deal) arrived in the Diamantina Shire's iron dinghy. Blue Mouldy was also the official Shire boat man for Birdsville, when the occasion demanded it.

Loading everyone and some of the gear, we set off for Birdsville, around six kilometres away. The new Publican and family were about to be delivered by boat!

After about an hour we came to the main channel of the Diamantina, crossed it, and headed along (or above, to be more accurate) the road into Birdsville, the extreme top end of the Birdsville track. We motored up to the back fence of the A.I.M. 'Hospital', and tied up. I went for a walk and lined up a vehicle to transport all and sundry to the pub.

Leaving the Nicholls to settle in, (they were to live on site, whereas Len Gaffrey and family lived in a separate house on the other side of Adelaide Street) I went to have a talk with Len. He was about to give me some advice, which I could either ignore or take on board. He told me that the current policeman's wife (who was working part time behind the bar) was carrying out certain practices which were not necessarily conducive in helping the pub turn a profit at the end of the year – not his words, but that was the message. He suggested that I sack her.

The other item concerned a couple of licensing inspectors, who never paid for their grog or accommodation. Len suggested that as a 'new broom', so to speak, I had the opportunity to clear both of these situations up. I fully agreed. At that moment, both the policeman's wife, and the licensing inspectors were at the Pub.

I had a talk to Silvie, and gave her the opportunity to deal with the 'barmaid', and I would deal with the licensing inspectors. She was the official licensee of the pub, while Taffy was the manager. Sylvie agreed, and straight away walked into the bar and sacked the lady in question. Just told her that her services would no longer be required. I was outside when the 'barmaid' flew out of the pub like a fowl with its tail feathers on fire, with accompanying sound effects. I thought to myself, this will have ramifications later, and it did.

Next morning, I was in the bar, after breakfast, when the two licensing inspectors walked out of the pub, about to board the plane for Brisbane. I went up to them and said "I'll fix you blokes up now if you like". "What do you mean?" one of them said. "Your bill", I replied. "Come into the bar and I'll give it to you". They just stared at me, and then the one that was doing the talking, said "We don't pay for meals and accommodation". "You do from now on," I replied, and walked into the bar. They followed me in and you could have cut the air with a hacksaw. I had the bill ready, and put it in front of them. One of them bought out a chequebook, and in silence wrote out the required amount, tore it out of the chequebook, pushed it at me across the bar, and they walked out without a word. If a cartoonist had done something on this, he would have had steam coming out of their ears! I again thought, there will be ramifications here, and there were.

Several weeks later, I was again in Birdsville, this time with a party to operate a safari out to the Muncooney Lake in the desert on the Eyre Creek. I had previously taken up a six wheel drive ex American army Studebaker truck. These are a great beast of a vehicle that returns around four miles to the gallon, but I had a sort of love affair going with it. It had the original canvas canopy on the rear, and wooden bench seats along each side. What passengers lacked in comfort (plenty!) they hopefully made up for in great vision. That's how I explained it to them. Normally the weather is very predictable in Birdsville, which was a big factor when this vehicle was operating.

We set off for Lake Muncooney in the Simpson Desert, around a hundred kilometres away. When we had to start *jumping* sandhills, I began having serious doubts about getting to our destination. It had the original thick ply bar tread tyres, and even when pressure was reduced they still stood up pretty well. We had a few minor sand bogs, but with numerous tries at some sandhills we were making progress. By mid-afternoon we were almost there, but one extra large hill blocked our every effort to get over it. There was no working winch on this vehicle, and I camped that evening, knowing there was no way we were going to get to Muncooney in this vehicle. (Later on I replaced the bar treads [duals at the rear] with big single aircraft tyres, that were much better in sand.)

The next morning before I was reluctantly going to turn around and return to Birdsville, I switched on the radio receiver to see if there was any traffic for me. There was. A seventy word telegram from the Birdsville policeman. It was a ranting affair, alluding to the sacking of his wife from the pub, quite extraordinary. I'm sure most of the population of Northern South Australia, Western Queensland and half of the Territory had listened with interest! The telegram demanded that I return straight away to Birdsville. There was no way I would have complied with the unreasonable demand, but ironically, I had no option but to return to Birdsville. I intended going back, and returning with the Range Rover and Toyota wagon that Peter Coombes and I, with the party, had arrived in Birdsville with.

We reached Birdsville about mid-afternoon, and booked the party into the pub. That evening the pub was pretty crowded. It was a weekend, and apart from locals there were a number of tourists there as well. The overweight policeman was slouched on a stool in his usual place down the western end of the bar, and he observed me come in. I said to Peter that he better watch my back, as I was expecting some sort of trouble from this man. Legally I had done nothing wrong, but that wouldn't necessarily stop him from getting his 'pound of flesh'.

After about ten minutes he stood up and walking past me, muttered "I want to see you outside". Not good. My plan was not to get trapped in a corner with this individual otherwise I could end up 'seriously compromised!'

I knew I could run a lot faster than he could. I followed him out, where an extraordinary situation unfolded. We were in an area between the bar, dining room, the old weatherboard annexe and the street. The street had recently installed concrete kerbing. I mention this because it is relevant to what happened next.

The man in question turned around and began abusing me for 'getting rid' of his wife from behind the bar. It was a startling performance and despite my 'ricketty position', I could not help a certain fascination. As he abused me, he began walking backwards (a good sign regarding my physical wellbeing), and so as to hear him, I followed, keeping a respectable distance between us. He reached the edge of the kerb, and next thing he went arse over head into the gutter! It was at that very moment that one of the Aboriginal stockman poked his head out of the bar door, gaping in amazement at the scene. He turned back and shouted into the bar "Rex has knocked Cliff arse over head!" Next thing the man in question, staggered to his feet, hopped into his Toyota, and drove off towards the Police Station. Some of the bar crowd witnessed his exit, and for a minute or so I enjoyed possibly my grandest moment. But then I related what actually happened. Still, it wasn't a bad outcome. From that moment on the 'man in question' never raised the matter again, and a few months later had a transfer anyway.

Patti and I owned the pub for six years (1974-79). Although we probably accumulated a few grey hairs, we enjoyed mostly good times, with lots of laughs, and meeting some very good people along the way – even though I (in particular) only spent limited time there during bush trips, apart from looking after it each summer for a few weeks.

We were living at McLaren Flat at the time, when we decided to sell the pub. The worst financial decision I have ever made, it could be agreed. However to make really good money from the pub we would have had to live up there and run it full time. That meant the safari business would have suffered. We have always been more 'lifestyle' people than business people, and the decision wasn't too difficult.

So in late 1980 we decided to sell. At the time, there was a serious aviation-gas shortage, which meant for some time there were very few people flying in and out of Birdsville. That was a substantial part of the clientele. Anyway, for whatever reason the agents recommended we put the pub up for tender. We did so, and it was advertised. After several weeks the tenders closed and we had only one person tendering. A very well-known person. We accepted the tender which was nearly three times as much as we had paid for it, six years earlier.

The agents informed me that the deal had been finalised, and we thought that was that. But it wasn't. Next morning I was at my parents place in McLaren Vale, when I had a phone call from the current Birdsville policeman, a teetotaller and a very reliable person. He gave me the unwelcome news that there was a major fire at the pub the night before. He told me that it had been deliberately started, but that it would be impossible to prove. If it wasn't for Yaro Pecanek (Pec) from Oodnadatta, who happened to be staying overnight in the pub, it is likely the whole building would have burnt to the ground. He was there at four in the morning, organising a bucket brigade with local people, because the tap in the bar sink had been left on resulting in no pressure in the outside hose. The fire was able to be restricted to the bar area and the annexe accommodation, which burnt to the ground. A TV film crew who were staying at the pub were out on the street and filmed the episode, a story that was relayed all around the world.

When the 'smoke cleared' the purchaser jumped up and down, saying he 'wasn't going to buy a burnt out pub'. The agents told me this, and asked whether or not I wanted to go ahead with the deal, because legally, it was sold. We decided it was only fair to let him off the hook, and did so, but received no thanks for this.

Business at the pub was severely restricted for a while, but after a week or so Taffy and Silvie Nicholls (the leasees) were operating as a 'licensed premises' from the kitchen area. I make the point here that they certainly had nothing to gain by burning the pub down, just the opposite.

After a few months we sold to an Adelaide syndicate, which didn't last long. Eventually it was purchased by the Brook family (Birdsville) and the Fort family, and is still operated by Kim and Jo Fort. A lot of money was spent on rebuilding with the addition of a modern motel alongside. This was all very necessary to cater for the expanded number of tourists passing through Birdsville every year. The pub was faithfully restored to its original state, but greatly modernised without losing too much of its character. You could say that the main difference between when I owned it, compared to now, is the absence of numerous colonies of daddy longlegs!

Patti and I have no regrets. It was a great privilege to own a very famous piece of Australian heritage.

2

A CROSS COUNTRY DRIVE

GREAT VICTORIA DESERT

In June/July 1999 I operated a 45 day Camel Expedition in the Great Victoria Desert incorporating South and Western Australia (see *A Sea of Sandhills* in my book *Ten Thousand Campfires*). During that trek we located a fresh water soak in a salt lake system, and that evening dozens (maybe hundreds) of Bronze wing pigeons came to water there. Onithologically, a very exciting event. Certainly was for me, with Night Parrots never far from my thoughts. We couldn't possibly spend another day there, but the next night we were camped only about thirteen kilometres, as the crow flies, from that location.

A couple of hours after sundown we heard a bird call, like nothing I have heard before. By the time we dug out a small tape recorder, the bird had moved further away and we were unable to record it. On checking several different bird books, and going on their description of the Night Parrot's call, I was very sure that what we had heard was in fact that *holy grail* of Australian birds.

In July 2005 I was running a 4WD vehicle Great Victoria Desert safari, beginning in Kalgoorlie WA, and finishing in Adelaide. I would incorporate the *Bronze wing soak* in the latter part of the expedition.

We left Kalgoorlie with me driving my Oka multicab, while Darren and Fiona Wallace, with children Amber and Jack, were in their Toyota Landcruiser station wagon. Darren works with me on occasions, and both he and Fiona were on the second half of the 1999 camel expedition.

Driving north through Menzies and Leonora, we arrived in Laverton in the late afternoon. A mate of mine called Murray Thomas and his wife Denise lived here after selling their Minara Station. Murray was chairman of the local Shire council. He also ran a couple of small businesses including a local four wheel drive safari operation specialising in the western part of the Great Victoria Desert. Well located, because Laverton pretty well sits on the western edge of the desert.

I had organised with Murray to spend a couple of days with us, inspecting various rockholes (rock water holes) in the region. Murray's interests and expertise was more on the historical (aboriginal and European) aspect, while my main focus was on the flora and fauna, particularly the birds.

We had a mixed party, with various interests, and included a couple of good bushmen and field naturalists. Stavros Pippos, the landscape photographer, who had travelled a lot with me in the past, was on board.

Murray was all ready, and we drove until dusk, arriving at the *Mallee Hen Rockhole*, setting up camp in the vicinity.

Unfortunately this rockhole was dry, but the country surrounding it was interesting.

Next morning Murray ran Stavros to a location in the area, well before daylight. Stavros was able to take a particularly good photograph of a panoramic desert scene, so his day was made even before he had breakfast. Some days he may only take one or two photographs, some days none at all. At the time he was recording material for one of his large *coffee table* publications.

During the day, Murray took us to other locations in the area, including rockholes (one with water), and places of historic interest. The only moment I could have done without was an incident that occurred when travelling on a wheel track through heavy thick mulga bush. There was a sharp angle in the track that Murray in his smaller Toyota twin cab could pass. The Oka was a different proposition. I had to do a bit of *shunting* to get around the corner, and in the process I managed to break my side ladder (to the roof rack). Patti told me off for a couple of *utterances* that I uttered, and life progressed. Later that afternoon, Murray headed back to Laverton, and we camped on a nice mulga flat.

(At the end of this chapter I will detail an account of Stavros' return visit to the area with Murray (less than a month later) and an incident that occurred, where he undoubtedly saved Murray's life.)

The next couple of days we drove on a series of tracks through a great variety of country, getting us across to what is known as the *Connie Sue Highway*. Len Beadell, who has travelled with me on several occasions, put this road in with his construction crew in 1962 when I was on the newly developing Rawlinna Station.

Early on we passed a *bush getaway camp* on the edge of a small salt lake. It is used by a number of outback police in the Gold Fields region.

We were seeing quite a few Bustards (Plain Turkeys) as the Great Victoria Desert/Nullarbor region is their main stronghold outside of the tropics.

Suddenly our little *wheel track road* joined the *Connie Sue Highway* (named after Len and Anne Beadell's daughter) which was just a slightly wider wheel track road, having had a couple of grades in the last forty odd years.

Soon after, I pulled up at one of the regular (every five kilometres) geodetic survey markers. In most cases, these are marked with a star picket (dropper) and a cross of white washed rocks. Where rocks are scarce the *cross* is in the form of a deep trench (which soon sands up). In the middle of the cross sits a brass disc set in a concrete block. These are consecutively numbered. They give surveyors a fixed position for whatever work is being carried out. Originally they were put in by National Mapping, the main purpose being to give heights above sea level, and one of the more obscure purposes was to determine any movement in the earth's crust. This could be ascertained by taking *star fixes* every ten years or so. Anyway, enough of this technical guff – I'm qualified to write *bush stuff*, not science journals!

The reason I pulled up here was very unscientific. Back in the late sixties when I used to cart good McLaren Vale wine (in particular Kay Bros, d'Arenberg, and Pirramimma) around in flagons, I would fill the empties up with water from my camp up the track a bit. The flagons were buried in the middle of the crosses on the geodetic survey markers – one every 10 kilometres between my camp (Coolgubbin) and Seemore Downs Station which is about twenty eight kilometres north of Rawlinna on the Railway line. This, in case I broke down, or for whatever reason, had to walk for help. I had flagons buried north of my camp as well, to Neale Junction, and then east to somewhere beyond the SA/WA border. To borrow a famous Royal Flying Doctor saying, it was along the lines of my personal *Mantle of Safety*, sort of thing. Some readers may be wondering at the amount of wine we used to carry – certainly wasn't one trip! I was doing up to four trips a year in the Nullarbor/Central desert region in the late sixties early seventies, and probably took about three years to *lay my flagons down*. Pretty good way to recycle flagons I reckon.

Now, the reason I pulled up. I had been telling my travellers about the water, and said we would pull up for a *taste*. To cut this rambling section a bit shorter, in a *nutshell*, I couldn't find a single bloody flagon! If anyone ever checks these markers, they could be excused for thinking there is more echidnas in the Great Victoria Desert than on Kangaroo Island, and that certainly isn't the case. Very frustrating it was. I may be wrong, but after a couple of days thinking about it, I came to the following conclusion.

In the past thirty years or so since my mate Rod Campbell (Kybo Station) put down a number of bores in the Southern Great Victoria Desert region of WA for the Aboriginal landowners – there has been greatly increased vehicle traffic. I know only too well that traditional aboriginals notice things in the bush more than most white blokes tend to do. They would only have to have seen one flagon top poking out of the ground (I buried them sitting up) for the *rot to start setting in* – as it were. Aboriginals are probably best in the world at finding water in the desert, but even *blind Freddy* would get a guernsey here. I was a bit annoyed that my *desert water* legacy had evaporated, but had to smile at the mirth it must have caused amongst the *people*. At least no one can ever accuse me of not helping my fellow indigenous Australians!

An hour later we pulled up at what was left of *Coolgubbin Camp.* I had the lease (from the Laverton Shire) for eighteen years before the then Conservation and Land Management (CALM) department of Western Australia, contacted me with the startling news that my lease was *in the incorrect location.* Now, many of you readers have been the *victims* of this type of Government Department *approach.* I could write a bloody chapter on this, but I'm not going to – just a couple of *bottom lines.* CALM informed me that they were proclaiming a *Wildlife Reserve* in the Neale Junction region. I suspected at the time it was only last week's idea, but the tenor of their letter was that it had been on the drawing board for years – and that somehow Rex Ellis had plonked his ten acre lease down in the middle of it! One WA critic of CALM, at the time, remarked that they probably didn't recognise the Laverton Shire! Well, be that as it may, my *camp* was legitimate, even though the rental was initially only ten dollars a year.

After digesting that letter (I didn't own a shredder!), I contacted my *Member for Miscellaneous Items,* old *best man* and mate, the Right Honorable Graham Campbell – the member for Kalgoorlie. He managed to get me twelve months *breathing space* because although I didn't intend wasting time, energy and money fighting it, I did have some infrastructure on the block.

I duly contacted the department, and asked them to offer me a price for the two 3,785 (1,000 gallon) litre tanks, water trough and roof catchment, not to mention the rain gauge. They answered, saying they were not interested in buying my improvements. I wrote again saying that if they were not going to compensate me, then I would remove them. That caused a hell of a stir! They reckoned the *people* were relying on my rain water. The way they carried on you'd reckon they were expecting a dozen *perishes* a year to be the result. What a mob! They must have thought I was some sort of public benefactor. I established that water there partly for my own use, but also to set up an artificial water point in a waterless area, with bird observations in mind. One thing I established, beyond any doubt, was that when thousands of Budgerigars were nesting in the area, green spinifex (Triodia seed) was their entire source of moisture. Some trips I spent a number of days camped in the area. Not once did I see Budgerigars coming to my trough. Long before feral camels proliferated, *travellers* shot the tanks full of holes. I was no longer using the camp regularly, but resented the arrogance of CALM.

Having stated that I was going to retrieve my assets, I had to do something about it, so with a mate (Des Stone from Willunga) set off in my 4WD *Blitz* camel truck. We drove over to Cocklebiddy – the camels travelled almost as fast as this truck – on the Eyre Highway. Our route then was by a series of tracks up to my old stamping ground of Rawlinna. This trip had three goals. Number one was to go to the *Rawlinna Muster* (Race meeting), number two was to go north to Coolgubbin and load up my *improvements,* and number three was to drive via Neale Junction, then west to Laverton before turning south to Goongarrie Station. I had arranged to give Len Johnson (*Two Mile Sheedy*) the improvements, and he in turn would give me a load of mulga posts. (He was the only licensed mulga post contractor in the world – the 1,036 square kilometre (400 square mile) Goongarrie station was pretty much *wall to wall* heavy mulga. It is now a conservation park.)

I only achieved two out of the three goals. Just as the Blitz rolled through the Rawlinna netting gate (the venue is located close to the town of Rawlinna on the vast Rawlinna sheep station) I heard a little *click,* and the vehicle lost power. It was a broken rear axle – the damage had probably been done thousands of kilometres earlier with a load of camels in an off road situation, but at least the Blitz delivered us to Rawlinna – well almost, we walked the last few hundred metres!

While we spent several enjoyable days there, with much use of the telephone I managed to get two axles on the way from both the east and west. Due to the good old Commonwealth Railways (as it was then) both lots passed through without stopping! As this little drama was in progress, there was a big dump of rain to the north, rendering travel to Coolgubbin camp impossible. So my *improvements* were going nowhere fast.

Des and I headed west along the east west railway line for what was to be my slowest ever trip to Kalgoorlie. We had taken the other rear axle out, so were driving in front wheel drive which didn't improve the steering with this vehicle. The six hundred kilometres via Kalgoorlie to Goongarrie Station, which is south west of the town of Menzies, took us a big two days.

After a long hard day (but enjoyable) cutting mulga posts with *Two Mile Sheedy*, and a good time with the Johnson family, Des and I drove back to Kalgoorlie and loaded the Blitz on a railway flat top bound for Port Augusta. Managed to round up one of the new well-travelled axles to throw behind the seat of the Blitz, before boarding a coach back across the Eyre Highway to Adelaide. I kept some of the mulga posts for myself to be made into furniture later on, selling the rest to an Adelaide wood turning group, which pretty much covered the costs of the trip. Enjoyable little jaunt, but frustrating that I couldn't collect my items from Coolgubbin.

Pulling up at Coolgubbin on this occasion was a marked difference to the last time I was here. If you didn't know it was here, you wouldn't know it was here. A bushfire had been through the previous summer, and the beautiful parkland of Marble gums (*Eucalyptus gongylocarpa*) were now timber skeletons clothed in a thick cover of bright green leaf growth, on a floor of green spinifex regrowth around 15 centimetres high. Some of the clumps of broad leaf mulga (*Acacia aneura*) had been killed by the fire, and there was no sign of the tanks, trough and roof catchment – just as though they had never been there. The bullet ridden tanks and the rest had probably been removed by the department. A sorry end to what had been a worthwhile project, I would have thought. Arrogance and stupidity cause a lot of grief in the world.

This would probably be the last time I would camp here (lunch on this occasion) but I had some great memories of this area, in particular, the numerous sightings over the years of Scarlet chested and Princess parrots – those two *desert specials*. When originally set up (see my book *Bush Safari*) in January in 1968 it was the only lease and *camp* in the Great Victoria Desert, both sides of the border. Bearing in mind that the Aboriginal settlements of Cundalee and Warburton are on the southwest and northern edges of the desert.

The next few days were relatively uneventful as we travelled via Neale Junction, and then east along the Anne Beadell Highway. With increased traffic over the last twenty five years or so this track is mostly badly corrugated, but with the Oka's tyres running at 35 psi we were hardly feeling them.

A relatively new addition to the area was the aboriginal owned Ilkurlka Roadhouse (WA side of the border) – a well-run operation, where we topped up our fuel and water.

In the vicinity of the state border, we left the road and it would be nearly a week before we would see another wheel track. Shortly after due to the Oka's weight (we weighed seven tonne all up when leaving Kalgoorlie) I became bogged in a bad patch of copi (powdered gypsum) but Darren soon pulled me out backwards with a *snatchem strap* – another very good Aussie invention. Copi is usually associated with inland saltlakes, and in the Great Victoria Desert the two dominant species growing in it are Black Oak (*Casuarina glauca*) and a number of Mallee (multi-stemmed eucalypt) species. Understory species and groundcover are often very scarce, sparse or missing altogether. Camp that night was in interesting country with a mixture of Mulga, Mallee and Black Oak and a varied shrubland.

Away next morning good and early. Our general pattern of travel was that Darren would select the route of least resistance, with Fiona on the GPS. I could then follow his wheel tracks in the larger Oka, deviating where necessary. Early on, a light rain began falling, which was annoying, although after a while it helped in the deeper sand.

Around mid morning we came across a limestone rockhole complex, consisting of three holes averaging about half a metre in diameter. In this instance they were all dry, but if this rain persisted that could change. They were located in a slight hollow on an open sheet of limestone the size of a basketball court.

Around midday I felt my rear side tyre go flat, and pulled up on the flattish top of a large sand dune. At the time I wasn't carrying any of the *goo* that makes most *flatties* an easy job these days, so we pulled it off over lunch and did a gaiter mend on the inside of the tyre. Not ideal, but would do for a spare.

I was taking a bit of a risk only carrying one spare, due to the very large load I was carrying. The big XDE Michelin 19.5 radials that I use are a superb tyre, and I rarely get a flat on or off road. If I was in dire straits this trip, for whatever reason, I had two lots of mates that would do an express run to me for assistance. You can't beat that sort of *roadside assistance*!

Mid afternoon, in the rain, we arrived at the site I call *Bronze wing Flat* on the edge of a large salt lake complex. The dune fields suddenly stop, and you have a drop of around 45 degrees sloping down to a large samphire flat, with the salt lake shining in the distance about half a kilometre away. We backtracked a few hundred metres to a huge spreading Marble Gum and set up a base camp, complete with a *hootchie* (Tarpaulin Cover) with rain threatening.

First off though, Darren, Collin, Bill Stav and I walked down to the flat, but to our great disappointment there was no water at all in the samphire channels, in particular where the Bronze wing pigeons had been watering on the camel expedition. It seems that the severe drought conditions had been enough to deplete it. Can't help bad luck.

The next day the rain had stopped (after about 20ml) and we did a lot of walking both in the dunes and around the salt lake. Colin did a lot of his close up photography that he has a flair for, taking anything from small leaf patterns, to insects, spider webs, you name it. A generally relaxed, pleasant day with good bird sightings, but nothing out of the ordinary.

I had hoped to follow the lake system south, but I walked for a couple of kilometres with Don and Patti and came across a nasty little situation where the salt lake came in close to a huge white sand dune. I would have bogged badly (nothing much worse than salt lake bogs) and been unable to turn around, so gave the lake idea away.

Instead, the following day, we took a bearing where a transect of around thirty kilometres would bring us out at a point where we may be able to cross the lake system. There was a feature that Murray Collins had visited a few years earlier that he called *Red Banks* – he had approached it from the south. We arrived at the spot, and after a reconnaissance on foot, found a narrow peninsula of sand that should allow us to cross. Before doing so we all fanned out on the samphire flat, as we had done at *Bronze wing Flat,* and *beat* the country for birds, hopefully of course for Night parrots. Nothing of note except a brown Songlark and a pair of Banded Plovers (lap wings). We duly crossed it without any problem, and continued on for several hours, to the south west, before arriving at Red Banks with three hours of daylight up our sleeve. It was indeed a dramatic location. From a high dune field to the south, the copi sand plain country sloped down to a saltbush/samphire flat, ending in a line of red clay/dirt *cliffs* about 6 to 9 metres high. Unremarkable in other circumstances, but out here it was a *feature of interest.*

A good afternoon walking around. That night after the evening meal, Bill Stav and Colin went for a walk. Bill had his very large flashlight and hoped to put up Quail. Both these two are keen and accomplished *birders.* They had only walked a couple of hundred metres from camp when they spied in the light, a very large bull camel in season, walking towards them. They turned and fled. Collin soon outdistanced Bill whose talents don't include running the four minute mile! He waited for her him to catch up, and they both sort of came to the conclusion that the camel just happened to be walking in that direction anyway! They were relieved, and we had a good laugh when they arrived back.

Next morning, heading south east, we cut a faint overgrown wheel track that probably led to Forrest Lakes. Years ago I remember a prospector mate of mine from Kalgoorlie (Johnny Carlisle) used to drive out here in his ex British army 4x4 Humber. He bought a lot of honey opal out of the area – not valuable, but usually an indication of the presence of opal. I would like to have gone to the Forrest Lakes (Western Australia), but unfortunately time did not permit. We were in country that had been burned a year or so ago, and had to keep a good lookout for burnt mulga stakes, which are deadly on tyres. After twenty kilometres or so we came out of the burnt country, passing into delightful Mulga/Black Oak, Bullock Bush and Blue Bush, and other ground cover. We did some walking, but didn't put up anything of note, and late that afternoon arrived at *Boundary Dam,* a feature discovered by Earnest Giles years ago. One of the rare occasions where aboriginals had made a *dam* to conserve water off a small claypan. Now it was hardly discernible, being almost eroded away. Nowhere near as good as the one we visited, a year later in this desert, south of the railway line on the camels (see *Go with the Flow*).

Next morning a heavy fog was on us, which gave the country a surreal feeling. At one stage we saw a string of feral camels, looking *ghostly* as they drifted away into the fog. A memorable moment.

Several hours later we arrived at the east-west road we were aiming for, completing our cross country segment. Well worth it, but always something of a relief to get on a *recognised road.*

A day or so later we were on the Eyre Highway, and heading for Adelaide. No luck with Night Parrots, which is an ongoing obsession of mine since rediscovering them in 1979 (see *Bush Safari*), but an experience that everyone thoroughly enjoyed.

A LIFE SAVED – AND THEN LOST

An account by Stavros Pippos

This brief introduction to Murray and his willingness to assist me on that very cold morning prompted me to contact him on my return to Adelaide and ask if he would be interested in accompanying me on a photographic expedition back into the Great Victoria Desert. My initial journey on the "Night Parrot Expedition" with Rex was not as photographically productive as I had hoped because of rain and cloudy days. Murray was a councillor at Laverton and said that provided he could be back for a council meeting in about two weeks he was very happy to accept my offer. I immediately flew to Kalgoorlie and then by bus to meet Murray at Laverton on Thursday August 3rd 2005.

Thursday 4th

Murray knew the Great Victoria Desert and was held I high regard for his knowledge of this wonderful desert. On this first day we visited many rock holes and places of interest ending with a return visit to the "Mallee Hen Rockhole" which unlike our first visit now contained water. Late afternoon I set my tripod in readiness for an early morning photograph. As we were descending the rocky ridge Murray casually told me he was an insulin dependent diabetic. Having a daughter with this same condition I have considerable experience of its consequences and I therefore asked him what medication and emergency supplies he carried with him. Like most men, Murray was reluctant to discuss the matter and brushed it off saying his diabetes was well controlled and there was no need for concern. Once we reached his 4WD I asked to see what medical supplies he had in case of an emergency and after we got over his initial reluctance he delved behind the back seat to reveal a dilapidated army bag in which was a glass of glucose, syringes and insulin. I understand he had a pump device attached to his belt from which insulin was automatically injected to his body on demand. I was at least happy to know what was on board although I could only take his word that he was well controlled and unlikely to suffer a Hypo induced coma as a result of low sugar.

Friday 5th

Plumridge Lakes was our destination but daylight was running out so we made camp overlooking Lake Raison. Murray set his tent near his 4WD and I on the other side some thirty metres away. The 2005 Ashes tour was underway in the UK and was being broadcast live even out there in the Great Victoria Desert. Murray had his radio on with the volume set very loud which kept me awake until well after midnight. The commentary was suddenly interrupted by a tirade of abuse coming from Murray's tent, this was followed by heavy groaning noises as if he was in severe pain. I naturally became alarmed, this was not normal behaviour and I feared he was in serious trouble.

The temperature was below freezing but I launched out of my warm swag and with bare feet raced towards Murray's tent and unzipped the fly to find him slumped unconscious against the canvas. Murray was a big man and it was impossible for me to lift or move him, at this point I didn't know whether he had suffered a cardiac arrest or was in a coma because of low sugar. My reaction was to get his army bag from the 4WD and get glucose into his system which proved more difficult because of the cold. The glucose was rock hard so I had to chip piece by piece onto a spoon and with his jaw prized open scrape the glucose across his teeth where it would slowly melt and find its way into his blood stream. If he was having a Hypo this would eventually bring him around. In the meantime I returned to my swag and got into warm clothes and boots then lit the fire and made a cup of tea to contemplate my predicament.

Should he not regain consciousness I faced the daunting task of getting help into a very remote part of Australia because it was unlikely I could lift him into the 4WD and if I could the nearest landing strip I knew of was many hours away over very rough terrain. I kept returning to his tent and eventually he mumbled that he felt very unwell, he complained he couldn't move his arms. At least he seemed to be regaining consciousness and I could see some slight arm movement. I returned to the fire and soon after he appeared from his tent asking me why I couldn't sleep having no recollection whatsoever of the drama of the past few hours.

The remainder of our long journey continued without incident although my nights were spent with one ear listening for strange or loud noises. Murray was the perfect companion with an encyclopaedic knowledge of the Great Victoria Desert and beyond, he was a genuine Australian bushman. We had discussed further expeditions but unfortunately several weeks after I returned to Adelaide I was informed that Murray had died.

AUTHOR'S NOTE (Rex Ellis)

Soon after Murray returned from this trip, Denise had to go to South Australia for treatment for her back condition. Murray was batching in Laverton. Several days later a neighbour found Murray dead in the house. A tragic premature end to an exceptional person.

MURRAY THOMAS

Murray Thomas was a good mate of mine, and is sadly missed.

I first met him when he and wife Denise owned and ran Nullarbor Station, on the South Australian side of the Nullarbor. It wasn't ideally suited for sheep (it is now part of the Nullarbor Conservation Park) as there was next to no water on the place, so Murray and Denise operated a very profitable little fuel stop, garage and café (Roadhouse). Unlike the modern Nullarbor Roadhouse/Motel complex, this was located a couple of kilometres north of the highway, near the little stand of Tuart Gums, arguably the Nullarbor's best known landmark.

Murray had given me valuable help in routes and attractions in his area, when I set up my first 4x4 Nullarbor safari (see *Bush Safari*)

A few years before he sold Nullarbor and bought Minara Station out of Leonora (WA) he asked me to come over for a few weeks and run the roadhouse (a very small affair then) while he and Denise were away. It was summer time, and my offseason, so I readily agreed. I'll just mention here one particularly amusing incident that occurred while I was there.

The only facet of this little gig that I wasn't real enamoured with was the truckies air horn that was wired up under my bed. There was a red button at the fuel bowsers, with large letters that said RING FOR SERVICE (24 HOURS). Even with the deplorable condition of the unsealed Eyre Highway as it was then, you would get tourists and others, rattling their tortured way across the potholes, corrugations and kilometres long *wallows* of bulldust, going both east and west at all hours of the day and night. Most of them looked upon the Nullarbor roadhouse as *the promised land* – an oasis in a desert of misery.

So after a hard day's work (it was usually pretty *full on*) I would be looking for a good night's sleep, which was to prove about as rare as a Nullarbor Quail thrush. I would be in a dead sleep, when this blast of sound from under my bed would propel me toward the ceiling.

Another rare species was a traveller that would just give it one little short *blast.* Most of the ignorant sods would keep a digit jammed on it trying to outdo that little Dutch bloke with his finger in the hole in the dyke – at least he was attempting to save his Nation, and not destroying forever the hearing and nerves of one of its citizens! Finally I dragged my swag to another part of the building to gain a bit of distance from the impact. I didn't want to disconnect it, because Murray probably would have lost a bit of business if the customer didn't have to have the fuel. I reckon it would have been a far more successful extractor of information than *waterboarding* currently is.

Anyway, I was doing something not real important one hot day when I saw a *semi* driving in off the road, trailing the usual great cloud of bulldust. It pulled up out the front, the driver door opened and the driver in a pair of baggy khaki shorts and a faded blue t-shirt sort of *sagged* down from the cab and collapsed in a heap on the ground. He was in a hopeless state of uncontrollable mirth! He laughed and laughed until he was *laughed out.*

Finally, he propped himself up against the front wheel of his prime mover, and related to me a little story.

He was driving along the *goat track called the Eyre Highway,* about twenty kilometres west of Nullarbor Station. In front of him was a Ford F100 towing a large cabin cruiser (boat) on a trailer. The Ford came to a half a kilometre long bulldust *hole* that had become full of water after recent heavy rains. There was half a kilometre of water, some of it around 60 centimetres in depth. The Ford had pulled up, obviously contemplating the scene ahead. Slowly, the rig entered the *waterhole,* and proceeded slowly along.

The truckie followed close behind, and watched as the F100 and large boat trailer *climbed out* the other end of the stretch of water covered road, on to dry ground. It was quite a steep ascent of about a metre. To the truckies amazement (and delight!) the cabin cruisers fastenings came undone, or broke, and the large boat slipped back into the water! Not only that, it actually *floated,* and that was when the truckie more or less lost control of himself. He must have regained a bit of temporary composure, because he helped the driver of the Ford *drive* the boat back on to the trailer when he reversed back into the water. It didn't sound like the F100 driver was too amused by the situation, but it seemed like there was enough *material* there to keep the truckie going for years.

He reckoned he suggested to the F100 driver that he ought to *set up* there and run boat tours, but the other bloke wasn't impressed. Nor was his missus who, throughout the whole debacle, remained in the Ford staring straight ahead, and totally unamused by events. The truckie had her worked out – he reckoned that *Captain Eyre* had spent a fortune in buying the boat with the *other half* not actually seeing eye to eye with the purchase. Be that as it may, the truckie said that in forty years of driving around the Land of Oz, he had never seen anything that *broke him up* like this had.

Just visualising the event, sort of made my day as well. My only regret was that the Ford/boat combination hadn't pulled in for fuel.

Anyway this short stay at Nullarbor was just another *window* in my association with Murray over the years. I saw a lot more of Murray and Denise (Denise was a loyal and willing supporter of Murray's many diverse activities) in later years after they had sold Nullarbor and moved over to the west, buying Minara Station out of Laverton. Here, Murray was able to enthusiastically indulge himself in the pastoral industry, which was his great love. It was only after he sold Minara to a mining company and moved into Laverton, that he started his own outback safari business. Being a natural bushman with a retentive memory, he soon accumulated a loyal group of clients. At the same time he was heavily involved in local government, holding the top job in the Laverton Shire for a number of years.

He had survived an event earlier, while mustering feral goats on Minara. He actually fell out of a low flying aircraft – knocked himself around, but survived that okay.

Less than two weeks after, Stavros had undoubtedly saved his life in the bush.

3
KALLAKOOPAH REVISITED

KALLAKOOPAH CREEK – TWO EXPEDITIONS (2009 AND 2011)

2009 EXPEDITION

My safaris to the north, when departing from my River Murray home, without exception, have two regular stops. The first is the Burra butcher owned and operated by Casey Cooper, and Hawker Motors, owned and operated by John Teague. Both give friendly efficient service, with Saltbush mutton the specialty of Cooper's Butchers and Hawker Motors described elsewhere in this book.

But getting back to the subject in hand. When I did the first journey down the flooding Kallakoopah in 2000, I thought it would be a *one off*. It is a desert river that specialises in sand and only carries water to Lake Eyre on very rare occasions. The Warburton Creek (river) has to be very high, enabling water to flood over a *sand bar* stretching several kilometres, and then to run into a series of channels heading deep into the Simpson Desert. It is very difficult getting boats into that system, and there is usually only a short window of time available before the Warburton stops, cutting off access to the Kallakoopah.

On this occasion I was to meet the party at the Mungerannie Pub half way up the Birdsville Track, as they were travelling there by four wheel drive and aircraft. The group of friends had been organized by Gerry Dickenson, an orthodontist, who had done a lot of off-road driving, and whose dream it was to one day travel down the Kallakoopah by boat. You could almost call it an obsession. There were two exceptions Peter and Kate Jenkins who had driven to our place and travelled up with us.

Two of my mates, Malcolm Hanson and *Spitta* Spitskosky (both good bushmen) were the other two boaties.

The Mungerannie Pub, with hosts Phil and PamGregurke is an excellent place to get to meet your party, and after a fun night we headed off next morning for Kalamurina Station. *B.J.* Smith had the aircraft and he left about the same time, intending to leave his Beechcraft Musketeer at the Cowarie Strip. Sharon Oldfield who owns and operates Cowarie was in the Pub the night before, and B.J. and she had made arrangements for a short flight to inspect cattle on the other side of the flooding Warburton. That was completed, and B.J. was picked up from Cowarie airstrip as we drove through.

Kalamurina had recently been purchased by the Australian Wildlife Conservancy, and after undergoing a hosing down of vehicles on a concrete slab, we drove out to a location where we would leave our vehicles and depart from in the boats.

The departure took longer than usual. The outboard I normally used for a number of years was a 15 h/p Yamaha four stroke. We normally use two strokes, which are a lot less complicated than four strokes. On this occasion it wouldn't start. Dead as a maggot. So it was *pulled down.*

Malcolm is a qualified mechanic, and a good one, and Spitta is a good *bush mechanic,* but after half an hour there was no solution to the problem. B.J. Smith had been an interested observer in the situation, and it turned out that he found the fault.

On the subject of B.J., his *flight path* through life has been an interesting one. He had recently retired after fifty years with Qantas, their longest serving pilot. He still spends a lot of time in the air in his *Musketeer,* and some of the places that aircraft had been landed, are not going to be recorded here.

So we finally got under way by three pm, heading up river. We were towing one of my old 3.6 metre (12 foot) flat bottomed punts full of extra fuel. It was one that I had used in 1974 when we crossed Lake Eyre.

It was soon apparent to me that it was a far bigger (higher) river than 2000. That was good, because I was concerned that our *window of opportunity,* in regards to getting into the Kallakoopah, was almost shut. I wanted this trip to leave earlier, but it just wasn't possible for the party to get organised sooner. Camped that night, and a great atmosphere in the group – anticipating the *grand adventure.*

Fast flowing water, and camped well short of the junction with the Kallakoopah, and it wasn't until 1:30pm the next day that we reached the area of the junction.

After lunch we started searching for a channel that could get us into the main *feeder channel* to the system, but soon encountered low water. Much less than 2000, and I was very concerned that we were indeed a week or so too late – the river had *gone.* There was plenty of pushing boats. Lots more reconnaissance in boats and on foot. Then Mal, Spitta, B.J. and I tried a likely channel leading off from the Warburton that was full of overhead Cooba. Did a bit of work with saws for a few hundred metres, before reaching more open water. Started looking good, but after about two kilometres we ran out of navigable water. We walked along it for half a kilometre and climbed a high sand hill on the edge of the channel. In front of us was a large body of water, or more correctly, where a large body of water had been recently. I spent ten minutes with my binoculars, assessing the situation, and came to the realisation that I couldn't risk attempting it. With the water dropping all the time, we could very easily become stranded, unable to progress or return, always one of my nightmare scenarios on these operations.

We returned to camp and gave the party the bad news. Gerry Dickenson was particularly despondent. Unbeknown to me at the time, he was very sick, but he had a great spirit and I was certainly unaware of it.

The plan, if unable to get into the Kallakoopah, had been to run the Warburton down to Lake Eyre and return, a wonderful trip, but not the *holy grail* of desert boat expeditions. But while travelling back to give the party the news, I had decided to try out an idea that was in the back of my mind. On the 2000 trip, only careful navigation had saved us from going down a fast watercourse (Tumapawarrina Creek) which led back to the Warburton – one of two creeks that do this. I told the party that we could have a go at accessing this creek from the Warburton, and following it against the current, back up to the Kallakoopah. The cautious side of my nature (the one that often gets overruled) told me to forget it, because stranding was a huge risk here, with a falling river – this *creek* water can drop heaps quicker than water in the main rivers. Everyone was in agreement, which was irrelevant really, because I had already decided to give it a go. Gerry, in particular, looked like he had a new lease of life.

After *smoko* we headed off, back down the Warburton, making a good pace with the flow. We saw a Black Falcon and a Black Breasted Buzzard, both iconic Australian raptors. Both species we usually see out here, but first for the trip. After some trouble we located one *floodout* of the Tumapawarrina Creek. I told Mal and Spitta to wait while we tried out the access in my boat. Initially, it didn't look promising.

The channel here averaged about forty metres wide, and was full of low bush, mostly Cooba. It was all scrub bashing, with the saw being used on occasions. It alternated between fast flowing deep water, and us running out of water.

After half a kilometre I pulled up and called the blokes up on the UHF radio. I said to "come up, we're on our way", with more confidence than I felt. When Mal and Spitta reached me, we got going again, with no sign of improvement. I think the party were wondering what they had let themselves in for. We just told them to "duck their blocks and keep their limbs inboard". But the often deep, fast flowing water gave me a fair bit of optimism. When we had covered an estimated three kilometres of heavy bush bashing, we suddenly emerged into a beautiful waterhole. The contrast was extraordinary. On our left hand side, at the bottom of the waterhole was a twenty metre high steep white sand hill, with live sand down to the water. The seemingly blue waterhole was lined with ancient low gnarled Coolibahs.

To look at them, you got the idea that it had been a long time between drinks in this neck of the woods.

It would have been a good camp, but because we were behind schedule I couldn't afford an early camp – the fact that the water in this creek could revert to sand just about overnight, was also on my mind.

The waterhole was over a kilometre long, and much enjoyed, before we motored into a massive lignum swamp. The next couple of hours was a combination of pushing boats through low water and running out various channels. Our navigation consisted of me *following my nose,* and Mal using his laptop map.

Technology is a great asset these days that I didn't have in the past, but it's only an aide, and not always applicable to the situation. Very often where to go just comes down to your instincts. The best guide of all is *flow* or lack of it, and one of the best tonics you could possibly have is being in a lignum swamp, or on a vaste flat full of low inert water, and suddenly finding a *flow*. Then, following it, and getting into yet faster water. Yeah, that's heady stuff alright.

We were fast running out of light, and it was almost dusk when we reached a solid shore of low tumbled white dunes. Not all that aesthetic, but open ground to camp, enough wood and deep water to moor the boats.

Next morning we were away by six forty am and had beautiful reflections in the swamp. The terrain was thick lignum, with channels and areas of open water, with water birds everywhere. Coolibah and River Cooba were scattered throughout, and much of the time we couldn't see land. We were following a fairly well defined channel most of the time, but not as much as the map would have you believe. Still we made good time with water becoming deeper and still fast flowing. The channel became more consistent, with some beautiful areas of white dunes cascading down to the water line. Around midday we had a very damp lunch camp near an old fence, very close to the Kallakoopah.

After lunch we were in the river, a big fast flowing body of water. The channel was about thirty metres wide with Coolibah covered flats full of water each side. It was only a kilometre or so up to the ruins of the long abandoned Mona Downs outstation, part of Cowarie Station. We had a look without landing. From here, we were only about fifteen kilometres in a straight line from the start of the Kallakoopah where we were a couple of days before. Everyone was hugely relieved (especially me!) to finally be in a river that was going somewhere. This relief however, soon changed to a degree of frustration when we arrived back down near our lunch camp. The channel split up into several, and on following different ones they all ended on the flats in shallow water with no flow. The situation bore no resemblance to how I recalled the river in 2000. It was as though the channel had suddenly gone underground. Mal's sophisticated computerised map only seemed to get us into more strife (and he was an expert in its use). Finally, after a couple of frustrating hours, which included climbing a sand dune for a look, we found ourselves in a new channel. Not only that, it was going in the right direction with increasingly fast flowing water. In half an hour it became a fair dinkum river, a channel from fifty to nearly a hundred metres wide. Encouragingly, it had banks both sides, or most of the time, with numerous floodouts with Coolibah covered flats to the horizon.

We made nearly thirty kilometres, before we came across a small tributary coming in on the north side. I headed up this for half a kilometre and found a camp. It was just after four pm and quite warm. The bank was on average about two metres high. There were a few large Coolibahs scattered around what was a very open bare flat of hard sand. Enough Coolibahs to provide shade, although some were a bit distant from the camp – but I was here mainly as there was ample wood. I needed plenty to cook a roast, and to stock up because we would be running out of Coolibahs before we travelled much further. I needed enough wood to get down to Lake Eyre, then back up the Warburton to where the Coolibahs started again.

An interesting little *incident* occurred at this camp. If you wanted to give it a title, you would probably catalogue it under *Benevolent dictatorship and party discipline* – something like that. I am not exactly sure why, but for some reason several of the girls took exception to my choice of camp, and voiced their objection. Now, the thing is, I'm just not used to anyone questioning my choice of campsites! I mean, it's what I do for a living. Anyway, on reflection I was probably a bit sharp with my reply, making it known in very few words that "where I say we will camp, we will very definitely bloody well camp!" From my perspective, it was probably the leadership thing – you have to keep the termites out of the structure, otherwise it will come tumbling around your ears. Potential problems need to be nipped in the bud, and I've always been very conscious of this.

Hopefully, the exchange didn't leave any scars because I'm acutely aware that little things can become big things in the bush, but I guess a few people just saw another side of *good old easy going amiable Rex!*

But from this hiccup, things galloped ahead to a very memorable camp, for all the right reasons. When our big fire burnt down us blokes put a couple of Casey Cooper's saltbush mutton legs in the camp ovens, along with a variety of vegetables. This would take a couple of hours, and the *miracle hour* began a bit early with cold beers passed around. Followed by just a bit more than the usual allocation of quality reds and whites.

There was general relief all round that, all things being equal, we would definitely get to the dead heart (Lake Eyre) on this rarely activated artery of, what in this country, is referred to as *white water*. The conversation was lively and full of fun. Peter, retired from the diplomatic service, was always in good form, to the extent that B.J., a man of dry and ready wit, labelled him as *a man who can converse with kings and commoners*. And so the night went on. The roast was excellent as usual, and even the tinned fruit and vanilla rice cream had a gourmet taste to it.

A late one for us, being eleven thirty before the only sounds to be heard were the liquid murmurings of the Kallakoopah on its rare journey to the desert heart and a pair of *mopokes* going about their nocturnal business.

Away next morning by six thirty. If there were any hangovers, they were well disguised, with the whole party very bright eyed and bushy tailed.

A few swans, a wood duck *playing dead* on the bank, as they do, and a sparrowhawk flashing through the timber were some ornithological treats. Large buck bush (Roly Poly) covered many sand hills, a good indication of numerous summer storms a few months previously.

Ian White was another dentist in the party. I quite often go barefoot on these boat trips, and although your feet become good and hard, you do get the odd splinter. I had a beauty on this particular day. Someone said it was a *log*, and big enough to start the night's campfire! Anyway, Ian brought out one of his evil looking tools of trade, and had it removed in the flick of an eye.

After lunch we came to a feature I call *Twin Lakes*. The channel runs into it and forms a body of water about twelve kilometres long, and averaging a couple of kilometres wide. We had a lot of trouble here in 2000 (see *Boats in the Desert*) wading and pushing boats through freezing cold water, trying to find the deep water. The bottom (southerly) lake had a sand bar in the middle, that we eventually found our way through, but this time Google Earth, aided by Malcolm's laptop map (GPS) made it even easier. Or so the *technocrats* in the party said!

In the top lake (a narrowing of the water body is the link between the two) there is a small island of around two acres in area, and arguably the largest island in the Simpson Desert – when there's water in the Kallakoopah that is. Even when dry it's still an island of sand in a massive claypan. There is a small sand hillock at one end with a prominent nitre bush on top, with good sandy flatter areas below and a *beach* all round. Good deep (enough) water to get the boats right to the beach. So this was our camp for the night, and a spectacular one it was as the scene sank into a breathtakingly beautiful sunset.

I had a bit of fun at this camp. The past few years we have recommended people bringing head torches, which are a great advantage when camping, freeing the hands. However, though very convenient, they tend to be a *social disaster*. It's very difficult to get people to turn them off or down, when they are speaking to you. Especially women, because they seem to have to look at you whenever they talk to you. Fact of life. Anyway, with *training*, we manage to get the situation of being dazzled, reduced. But on this trip one particular lady (a lovely person, and I am sure this was her only failing!) was oblivious to the tuition in this area.

After nearly a week of stumbling around like a rabbit in a spotlight, I decided to take direct action, and told Spitta and Mal what I was going to do. We were all sitting on our camp chairs around the fire, and I made sure I had an extra large helping of my evening meal. I had eaten well over half, when I addressed the lady in question. She was sitting opposite me eating her meal with headlight on high beam as usual (most headlights have an infrared light as well, ideal for eating). Soon as I spoke to her up came her head, her searchlight hitting me right between the eyes. I gave a yell, and threw myself backwards, and as the chair and I went over I threw my plate into the air!

The good lady was horrified, and as I picked myself up off the deck, she was full of apologies. "It's okay", I said, "Your light got me right between the eyes". Amongst a fair bit of mirth, she really got the message, but being a smart aleck often has its costs – in this case, a broken chair, and I sat on my swag for the rest of the trip!

Next day was very windy, but we were almost off the lake before it strengthened. Plenty of orange and crimson chats along the shores. Only the odd stand and single Coolibahs to be seen now, and that night's camp a nondescript one in white jumbled sand dunes. Spitta located a number of aboriginal artefacts in the area.

Made a *big mile* the next day to keep up with our schedule. The size of the river, with the channel between one to two hundred metres wide with a very fast flow, was a subject of continual wonder. We were having smokos lasting only a quarter of an hour and half hour for lunch, which was a pity but necessary. After lunch we saw a huge bull camel running across the flat, kicking up a spray of water as he went. He was headed towards us, and I headed towards him so that people could get some photos. I got stuck on a *gob* of mud, and stalled my motor. Meanwhile the bull kept coming. As I feverishly worked on *unbogging* the boat, the camel actually entered the water of the river with the depth up to his knees before stopping thirty metres away. Some good photography was had. I like to think he was just curious.....

Just before we reached the northern most point of the river, we searched in vain for the Diprotodon leg that was protruding from the bank, about a metre of it. I had reported it to the SA Museum, along with photographs, and in their opinion it was a whole Diprotodon in situ. The water was a lot higher this year, and it would have been under water anyway.

Another very large lake (un-named) was in front of us, and as we were entering it from the channel, and pushing through more mud than water, Trevor Wright (Wrightair) flew over us.

He was a welcome sight, because I was expecting him to drop me a grease gun. We were having trouble with a secondhand motor on Mal's boat, and some grease would have made his life a lot easier.

However, it was not to be. Trevor told me on the radio that he had an airsick lady on board, and it wouldn't be possible to drop the gun. Never mind, it was a good idea. Trevor has always given us a lot of support over the years. His operation is based at Willow Creek, and they usually fly my party over Lake Eyre after the boat trip, giving people a great perspective of the trip.

That night a very spectacular and beautiful camp on a little bare flat at the foot of a fifteen metre cliff. An excellent mooring at the mouth of a small creek that ran into the river here. Up that creek a hundred and fifty metres was the remains of a massive wedge-tailed eagle nest that had broken the mulga that supported it. It provided us with some welcome firewood for the evening's campfire.

From here to the confluence with the Warburton things get a bit tricky. First thing, as the sun came up we motored along several kilometres of low cliffs, with beautiful reflections. Birdlife was good with numerous large Australian shell duck (the old *mountain duck*) and swans, some with nests visible. Then, a few channels where it is easy to go wrong. We were travelling through a dead flat landscape now, actually the floodplain of three rivers – the Kallakoopah, Warburton, and the Macumba – it comes in from the north with several *mouths*. They are all very narrow, around twenty metres wide. Here, like in 2000, we encountered a lot of mud and *mud rock*, washed down the Macumba, but not as bad as in 2000 when we were held up for a long time with low water.

We were now in a very narrow (ten to twelve metres) fast flowing channel with the water often only centimetres from the top of the bank.

Then the great moment as we entered the Warburton around eleven o'clock. On through the *lower broadwater* (my name) before motoring through the mouth of the Warburton into Lake Eyre, about one o'clock. This moment never fails to have a profound effect on people, and this was no exception. We headed on the several kilometres to what some people call *Ellis Island*, but what I call *Royal Spoonbill Island*, having seen a pair there one trip – a long way west for this species.

The magic of landing on the island was somewhat diluted by people having to stagger ten metres through nearly a metre of glutinous black mud. But I just told them that "mud is good", and they got on with it – except for Peter who fell over backwards and had to be extricated! Malcolm produced a bottle of excellent port that improved the situation no end, and fortified the party for the return trip. After lunch and the return to boats through the mud, we headed *up river*.

The next three and a half days had to be long ones, getting up at four thirty am and away by six am. We were using fuel now from my various dumps established in an earlier Warburton trip. Still lots happening all the time with dingo behaviour, birds and the great scenery the ever present attraction. The main ornithological highlight on this leg was an excellent sighting of a Square Tailed Kite. I quite often record them on the Warburton, but it is a rarely seen species.

Arrived at the Kalamurina landing on the afternoon of the twelfth day, having covered nine hundred and four kilometres – our longest desert boat trip.

2011 EXPEDITION

Two thousand and eleven saw the Warburton and Cooper running into Lake Eyre for the third year in succession which was pretty amazing, and the end of April saw us beginning a third Kallakoopah/Warburton round trip. This was to be of fourteen days duration.

Both rivers were even bigger than 2010. We had four boats as well as towing two inflatables full of fuel, with sixteen people all up. Not to mention my Jack Russell, *Billycan*. The *boaties* included Len Cooper, Rick Moore, Ron Goudie and myself.

Here are a few highlights from this trip, which began from Cowarie Station.

Once again we had an enormous amount of trouble getting into the Kallakoopah system. It seems that so much sand gets moved around this area, in particularly during floods, that what I learn on one trip is often irrelevant on the next. We lost the better part of a day pushing boats, trying different channels, etc. before finding fluctuating flows of water that was certainly taking us somewhere, but not all plain sailing. I would just begin to feel confident, and the channel would peter out on to flat with no flow. In a flat country with very few features and landmarks, extra water height can change the whole area beyond recognition.

Anyway, by late afternoon we were on a nice fast flowing channel, and I camped while we were in front. I don't like going to bed being *bushed*. Even the illusion that you are on the right track is better than nothing!

But next morning things only got worse and we found ourselves out on a huge flat of shallow water with no flow. I could see a smudge of thick Coolibah in the distance that I reckoned had to be the main channel before it reached the abandoned Mona Downs outstation. I told the party, that whatever it took, we had to get ourselves across to it. We were not going back.

With alternating sections of shallow water motoring with often more mud than water, and pushing boats, we were getting closer to the timber. Then, when our strength was almost depleted, we got into a bit of a channel that gradually deepened. It was becoming full of dead and live Coolibah and the saw was required. When it became almost impossible to travel I took my boat into shore and walked along it towards the thick timber. To my great relief, within about two hundred metres I came across a fast flowing channel of deep water that could only be *our channel.* I walked back with the good news, and in another half hour with much cutting of timber and manoeuvring boats around trees, we motored into our river. In ten minutes we arrived at Mona Downs and landed for lunch.

There was very little remaining to indicate that this place was ever inhabited. Some old farm machinery used for the growing of lucerne and the remains of old pig pens constructed out of heavy Coolibah. We had lunch near a few large Athol Pines and the remains of the homestead foundations. Our short lunch here turned out to be around one and a half hours, because Billy had disappeared down a rabbit warren. Normally he is pretty good with warrens (for a Jack Russell!), coming when I call him. But not this time. He did come up once for a look, but after a quick look at us, disappeared again. Ironically, it was the same warren that *Stubbie* had gone down in 2000 wearing the colourful woollen coat that Matty Reilly had given him and when he did come, he was minus the coat! The only good result here would have been if Billy had reappeared wearing Stubbie's old coat, but it wasn't to be. He finally emerged, coatless, and we continued on our way.

More trouble at the Tumapawarrina Creek junction. Even with Rick's GPS laptop map we were getting nowhere. The channel split into three, and after following two to no avail, we followed a meandering channel with less and less flow, before it also ran into nothing.

We pulled the boats up at a large white dune, and took our lunch bags up the top for a look around. We were surrounded by water on three sides. We could see where we had to go in order to cut our main channel, and after lunch we did just that.

Amazingly, we had only gone less than a kilometre, when we struck flowing water, quite deep, but in no discernible channel. Just dead and live Coolibah either side. We kept with it, and after a couple of kilometres we were suddenly back in the river. It's a weird and wonderful system.

This year, compared to an earlier trip on the Warburton, there was significantly more birdlife in the Kallakoopah – both in numbers and species, and the ornithology was a constant source of enjoyment down the length of the Kallakoopah, before dropping off to the drought affected numbers as we head back up the Warburton. Hard to understand considering the two watercourses' close proximity to each other. Presumably food was the key, but the country was pretty much identical, but with probably more biodiversity along the Warburton, due to the fact that it runs a lot more often than the Kallakoopah.

This was very much a *rat year* – that is, the country was full of the Long Haired, or Plague rat. Individually, a nice looking native animal of sandy grey colouring, with distinctive long black hairs on its lower back. Most of the time they exist in small pockets in isolated parts of the inland and tropics, their numbers occasionally exploding in successive good seasons. They certainly make life interesting when you are camped out. They can run across your head in the swag (insect domes or mozzie nets keep them out) giving rise to some 'dramatic exclamations' through the night.

Billy had a field day for a while, and when his paws became sore from digging them up, I had to tie him up. Some nights the squeaking can keep you awake. You don't see much of them in the day time, but before we retired for the night, our last job was to put edible food, etc. up on the tables out of reach.

Two species, in particular, breed up in extra large numbers during these irruptions – the Barn Owl and Letter Winged Kite. The latter being the only truly Australian nocturnal/diurnal raptor. On occasions further north in this desert we have watched them hunt with spotlights. Quite remarkable. It is rare to see Letter Winged Kites most years. When they reach large numbers they mostly nest in colonies, and there are records of colonies being greatly decimated by feral cats. It is very much an endangered species.

In these good years, when the *rats are running*, you hear Barn Owls calling through the night, and often put them up through the day. Both of these birds die off in large numbers when the Long Haired rats eventually run out of food after the seasons get back to normal. When the herbage becomes scarce, the rats start to cannibalize themselves and disease and natural starvation gets them back to *normal* numbers. Such is nature.

A few days went by making good time on a huge river. Most Australians have no concept of the amount of water that flows through northern South Australia in these special years – the *driest state in the driest continent* doesn't live up to its name on these occasions.

Twin Lakes was a lot easier to negotiate this year because of the extra water. We had well and truly *caught up with the river*.

This time just a quick lunch stop on the island. A day or so later and a few hours of passing the northern extremity of the river, we came across a mob of over forty camels that were feeding on a sand dune close to the river. Even though the country is full of camels, you can do a whole Cooper or Warburton trip without seeing any, as they have no reason to be near water. Particularly in the cooler months.

We were just about to take off again after our meeting with the camels, when I saw this large object in the water. At first I thought it was an oversized tyre tube, blown up, but on closer inspection, it turned out to be the bloated body of a very large Woma or Sandhill Python. These are considered rare, and with all my walking around deserts with the camels, I have only ever seen about half a dozen. This one was just under two metres in length, and had possibly been washed away with the first flood waters. Good to see even if it was dead. This specimen was large for the species.

All the time, lots of birdlife. So far two Square Tailed Kites, and a possible third, although couldn't be sure. Many raptors are particularly hard to identify due to the great variation in plumage of immature birds, and different colour *morphs* in some species. Big flocks of Hardhead ducks (our only fish eating duck), and a flock of thirty Pink-eared ducks – encouraging, because they were one of the species that had been decimated by the drought.

One night, while camped on flat ground opposite a sand cliff, some of us heard a loud *metallic boom*. Next morning, across the river from us, we could see where hundreds of tonnes of sand had broken away from the *cliff*, ending up in the river. Interesting.

Well behind schedule, so next morning we were away by 5:20am, boaties using our headlights. The first three operators had our head torches reversed on our hats, showing the red lights. A very effective way when the river is open, to make an early mile.

A night later, after two very long days, we were at *Royal Spoonbill Island* on the lake, arriving at sunset. Always a wonderful camp, and this one no exception.

After a sleep-in with a lazy breakfast of bacon and eggs, we loaded up (no mud this time, with a higher lake) and headed back up the Warburton.

Each time I have travelled the Kallakoopah, I have reckoned it will be my last. I'll just have to wait and see.

4
HOW TO MAKE A BREAD PUDDING

THE MOUNT ROSE CHARTER

In 1967 I had a charter with a mining company, called Mount Rose Mines. It was in the middle of that mini mining boom in the mid 1960's, and there was quite a bit of interest in the Flinders Ranges – both in reworking old sites and discovering new ones.

Mount Rose Mines engaged me for a period of six weeks in the winter of that year. My job was to cook for six mining blokes and act as guide. I had to drop them off in the morning and pick them up in the late afternoon from their area of operation. The area concerned were Mt Serle, Yankaninna, Umberatana and Mt Freeling Stations, in the Northern Flinders Ranges.

It was also my job to contact the stations and take care of any arrangements to do with the logistics of the operation. The company told me to purchase the *very best food* for the party and to bill them for it after completion of the contract. I quoted a good fee, it was accepted, and I felt pretty good about the situation.

I met the five mining blokes (all in their twenties) and *Haggis* Shackleton, the geologist, who was around thirty, in Adelaide. He was a wild looking bloke, a thatch of unruly hair, similar beard and horn rimmed specs, with a very robust and infectious laugh. We travelled up to Copley and then sixty three kilometres out to Mt Serle, right in the middle of the widest part of the Flinders. I had to see the owner, Jim Smith, to okay the survey on his property. The mining boys stayed in my Land Rover station wagon, and Haggis in his Mini Moke, while I went into the homestead.

I knocked on the door, and almost immediately it was opened by this attractive little blonde sheila, who I thought would probably be the Governess. I introduced myself and asked if Mr Smith was in. She (the attractive little blonde sheila) said "I'll go and get Dad", and disappeared. So she wasn't the Governess. Such was the effect that she had on me, when Mr Smith arrived I almost forgot what I was there to ask him. I explained the situation and he was very friendly and cooperative. When I showed him the mining sheet and explained the area we had to cover, he offered us the use of *The Weedna,* a stone hut used as an outstation.

Mt Serle was 497 square kilometres in area, its country stretching along the Frome Creek, the Flinders largest watercourse, and the only one that runs into Lake Eyre North. Weedna hut was up the top of the run, around thirty five kilometres from the main homestead. He said it would take us a couple of hours to get out there as the track was very rough. I thanked him and we departed soon after in the two vehicles. I didn't feel one of the hundreds of gutters, because my mind was on *the girl*. I knew I had a limited window of opportunity, as we would only be in the area for a week or two. I kept my thoughts to myself.

We arrived at the little stone hut just on dusk. We had travelled through some very interesting and beautiful Range country on the way from the Station, but Weedna was set in lightly timbered, almost bald hills, with a Ti Tree creek running past. It was an interesting setting with a very large Broughton Willow (Acacia) nearby. We settled in with the blokes rolling their swags around the verandahs and Haggis and I with ours on shearers beds in the *bedroom* next to the *kitchen/dining room.* Soon had the fire burning strongly under the boiler, and then hot showers while I knocked up a feed. It was the first day of a potentially exciting job, and there was a lot of animated talk. The mining blokes (field assistants) knew each other, Haggis and I were getting along well, and I was looking forward to the job. However I was very much preoccupied with my thoughts of Mr Smith's daughter, whose name I found out, was Patti.

Next morning I ran the crew out to a location about six kilometres from the hut, with Haggis accompanying us in his *Moke*. They were engaged in what is called a Geochemical Survey. Each man had a small section of map, traced off a larger geological map of the general region. These small traced maps showed every creek and gutter from the various high points in the area. Everyone had in his backpack, a number of small brown paper sample bags. Each man would walk to the highest point on his section of map, then begin walking down hill, taking samples from the junction of gutters, and then larger creeks, until finally the junction where they ran into the large gum creeks at or near the lowest point on their maps.

The principle behind this was that if there was a *mother lode* of some mineral higher up, it should show up in the samples at the junctions further down. As samples were taken their position was marked accordingly on the small maps for later referral if anything showed up in the laboratories in Adelaide, where they were analysed.

It was a very physical and comprehensive way of covering the country, and there was no way these men were not going to be a lot fitter at the end of the job. Most of them were city blokes, and as I was sort of responsible for them I had a few concerns about them getting lost.

After I dropped the boys off at their location, Haggis headed off to his own pursuits, and I drove back to Weedna hut. This was to be the pattern of most days. I would be back at the hut and make preparations for the evening meal, and then the rest of the day was pretty much my own. Giving me ample time to desperately consider my tactics where Patti Smith was concerned.

I made myself a mug of tea, and sat out on the verandah considering the situation. I needed to ask her out, or somehow get to spend a bit of time with her, but HOW. I know now that most blokes are piss weak when it comes to asking girls out, particularly in those days. These days, from what I can see, all the *social media* stuff available probably makes things a lot easier – you can have a full on relationship without even meeting the other person! Frightening, I reckon, but that's the way it is. Back then there was no alternative but to put yourself on the line, and blokes hate making fools of themselves. We are so bloody pathetic really. But the sexual male/female thing is so strong, that despite often deep reluctance we are unable to resist the urge to get involved. Which, for the sake of the species, is just as well!

I mean, if I had any guts at all I would just ring her up and ask her out to the pictures in Leigh Creek, on Saturday night. But I broke out in a cold sweat (it was a warm sunny morning) just thinking about it.

The phone was here, well sort of. It was a single line of fencing wire stretching from the main homestead to Weedna hut. No satellite phones or UHF radio back then. This wire ran mainly along the top of fences, many of them over a hundred years old. It crossed numerous gum creeks, running on or above flood gates until it finally arrived at this little stone hut. Despite the bad reception, there was the means. But I spent all that day unable to pluck up the courage to ring the girl. How pathetic is that?

About four o'clock I headed out and picked up the boys, and apart from one slightly twisted ankle they were all in good shape, though slightly *buggered* by the unaccustomed exertions. Haggis arrived back soon after, and we sat down to our evening meal. Before long everyone was in their swags, including me, and I was still wrestling with my *problem* when sleep claimed me.

In the morning I was up before the others preparing their lunches of sandwiches, cake and an apple or orange. Getting out of bed wasn't a strong point for most of these blokes, except Haggis, but they duly wandered in to breakfast. Afterwards, I took them out to another area where they would repeat their process of sampling.

Haggis was off on his own most days, engaged in geological mapping of the area, marking data on an enlarged aerial map that he had in the Moke.

It was as I was driving back next morning slowly, in 4WD low range along something that passed for a truck, that my brainwave arrived. I had a plan, albeit, a desperate one. I tried to push my old Land Rover a bit faster, in case my *courage* evaporated before I arrived back at the hut. Pulling up at the hut, I walked straight in, and gave some vigorous rings on the handle, then picked up the earpiece and waited, my heart in my mouth. My first fear was that Patti's mother would pick up the phone, which would throw me into a state of confusion. She would probably want to know what I wanted to talk to her daughter about. If that occurred I'd probably chuck the hand piece in the air, and rush out into the bush!

But no one came on the phone. Just a weird mix of jangling metallic sounds, and I quickly visualized trying to get a coherent message along that length of fencing wire with its dozens of figure eight joints – this is supposed to be the twentieth century for Christ sake! So I replaced the earpiece and gave the phone another series of rings, but what courage I had was taking a pizzling. There was the same loud background racket, but then, like a ray of sunshine through the gloom I heard this sweet voice say, "Hello, this is Patti." I nearly dropped the earpiece and made a huge effort to prevent my knees from dropping me to the floor. Then I launched into my miserable effort. "Good day Patti", I said, "This is Rex Ellis here – you might remember me, I called in the other day with those mining blokes." There was a lot of jangling noise on the line, and for a terrible moment, I thought she had hung up on me. Then, as if from somewhere in outer space, came her voice, "Yes, I remember you." "Ah good, look I'm wondering if you might be able to do me a big favour?" More jangling and then whistling noises on the line. Hoping she was still on the other end, I continued, "I'm cooking for these blokes, and they expect a fair bit of variety. I wonder if you would be able to give me a recipe for a bread pudding?" More racket as I waited with my heart in my mouth. After what seemed like forever, Patti's voice floated out of the racket, saying "I can tell you how to make a bread pudding – do you want to write it down?" "Yeah, I've got a pen and paper" (I didn't!) As Patti gave all the details of constructing a bread pudding, I wasn't listening to a word. I was trying to pluck up courage for the next rickety step in my devious project to establish a connection with this lady.

When the recipe was complete, I summoned up the last miserable drop of my courage and said, "Thanks a lot Patti, that should keep them happy – Er, look, I don't suppose you would want to go to the pictures with me on Saturday night?" More racket on the line that went on and on. Had she hung up? Probably. Either she had hung up, or gone away from the phone. I didn't know what was worse. Anyway after about a minute that seemed like an hour, she came back on. "I'll let you know when you come in on Saturday". I must have mumbled something back, and she probably hung up.

I sat down on a kitchen chair sort of shell-shocked. Patti knew I was coming in on Saturday to pick up our stores off the mail truck. She said she would *let me know* … … …. How cruel is that? Still, I was in with a chance, and could do no more. It was only Tuesday. I would somehow have to get myself through the rest of the week. Now, I've always been an optimist, so I psyched myself up to believe that she would say *yes*. The opposite didn't bear thinking about and I tried not to.

As the days passed I said nothing to the boys, and when Friday night came I told the blokes that I was going into the Station to get the stores and mail, and that I wouldn't be back until Sunday morning. I prepared lunch and the evening meal, and Haggis said he would take care of it. Thankfully, no one asked why I would be back so late, and I didn't think they were aware that Mr Smith had a daughter, and I certainly didn't let on. I left after smoko on Saturday morning, and had my swag with me in case of a *no*. If so, I intended on camping out and getting back Sunday morning no matter what the answer was.

I arrived at the Mt Serle homestead around midday and loaded my stores. Mr Smith had two sons, Jim and Ken. Ken was in Adelaide playing league football for Glenelg. Jim was very friendly toward me, and invited me to stay for lunch. About then, Patti appeared, and I attempted to affect a casual demeanor, even though I was undergoing some sort of interior meltdown. Women are not stupid in these matters, and she wasn't fooled (I learnt much, much later).

Lunch was a pleasant affair, and I was on my best behaviour as I was asked questions about what I did for a living, this job, etc. Patti wasn't saying much and I wasn't sure if that was good or bad. After lunch, like some sort of religious ceremony all and sundry moved out to the *sun room* on the verandah to listen to the football. Glenelg were playing Norwood, and Ken was playing in the back pocket. I was asked to accompany them, and Jim brought me a beer which I sorely needed. We sat glued to the radio, and I can't remember who won, but everyone was pretty relaxed, so I guess Glenelg did. Then, Patti asked me if I would like a game of table tennis, and of course I agreed. I would have agreed to anything she asked!

We played a couple of games, and then she put down the bat, looked me in the eyes and said "Rex, I would like to go to the pictures tonight." "That's good", I said, which would have been the understatement of the year! Patti disappeared, and Jim brought me another beer which I also needed, and we sat down and had a yarn about Mt Serle.

I sensed I had an ally in Jim (young Jim) and I was very grateful. I needed all the support I could get. After about half an hour Patti arrived in her *good gear*, and we were ready to go. We headed off with a minimum of fuss, and I thought – life can't get much better than this! Took about an hour. The Leigh Creek *flicks* was a very casual affair as you would expect. Actually held in a small *theatre*. After the show, of which I have no recollection, we went and had coffee with Hedley and Sue, friends of Jim and Ken's. Then we drove back to Mt Serle, the mood very convivial indeed.

When we came to the horse paddock gate, Patti hopped out and opened it, and I drove through trying to pluck up courage to attempt a *goodnight kiss*.

Yeah, that's the way it was, and no doubt there is a reader or two who would identify with the situation. She hopped back in and we drove the half kilometre to the homestead. As we pulled up, Patti leant over and kissed me on the cheek, saying that she enjoyed the evening. When I got my breath back I asked her if she would like to do it again on the following weekend, and this time she gave a positive *yes*. I drove off into the night a happy man.

It wasn't long before the boys *twigged* what was going on, and I was getting a bit of rubbishing from them, but it didn't bother me.

The following weekend there was almost a carbon copy repeat of the first occasion, except there was a slightly longer pause when I pulled up at the homestead.

Early the next week, we were finished on Mt Serle and moved camp to the Owiendana shearers' quarters on Yankaninna Station, the next run to the north of Mt Serle, owned by Dean and Beryl Lillecrappe. This was an old traditional building constructed of *pine and pug* and is now heritage listed. We spent a couple of days there, before we were to move on to another old stone boundary riders hut called Douglas Hut. This was out the back of Yankaninna, not far from the Frome Creek.

While we were at Owiendana, there was an unusual incident involving one of the blokes. I was picking each of them up in their different locations, and when I came to the spot where I expected to find Ian, he wasn't there. I left one of the others there while I went off and picked up the other two, and on returning, he still wasn't there. Here was a dilemma. It was almost dark by this time, and so I fired a couple of shots from my 32/20 rifle. We lit a large fire and waited another half hour, before going back to the hut, which was in the vicinity of an interesting feature called Mt Rose, (the hill/mountain that my employer was named after), and the present operations were around this area. After the evening meal I drove back to the fire, but no Ian, so I fired another couple of shots. In the end I gave it away, as we couldn't do anything until the morning. It was a very dark night – no moon at all.

Following day we all walked Ian's area of operation, but no luck. However when we widened our search, we came across him walking up a creek and looking in fair shape. He had a story to tell. Somehow (still not quite sure how), he had become lost, not being able to make his map *fit the country*. He had heard a shot but as there was a south westerly blowing at the time, he couldn't ascertain the direction. Realising he would have to camp out he found a large dead red gum lying on the bank of a creek. On inspection he managed to trap a half grown rabbit in it. Not having any matches, he actually ate it raw! He then lay down in the hollow tree, making himself as comfortable as possible and went to sleep, not that he got a lot of that. Full marks for survival instincts anyway.

Later in the week we moved out to Douglas Hut, which was nearly as rough and distant from Yankaninna homestead, as Weedna hut was from Mt Serle.

On Saturday morning I left the hut for Mt Serle (things were now *regular*) after having arranged for meals up to Sunday lunch. We didn't work on weekends.

When I arrived at Yankaninna homestead to pick up our stores I found that the Lillecrappes were taking a great interest in this little romance, Beryl especially. She suggested that after I dropped Patti off, I could camp for a few hours at the Owiendana quarters, which were midway between Mt Serle and Yankaninna homestead. Then I could come to Yankaninna for a hot breakfast before beginning the slow drive out to Douglas hut. Sure suited me. As well as grilled chops, I had to subject myself to a *grilling* from Beryl as well, as to the *state of the romance*, but I didn't mind that.

One day, half way through the week, one of the boys had to go into Leigh Creek to ring up. I gave him a small food order, which included a dozen tins of vanilla rice cream. When he came back that evening he had everything correct except one item. He had a dozen tins (containers) of vanilla ICE CREAM! Was he thick or what? I thought 'oh well, the company is paying for it', so I proceeded to serve vanilla ice cream in the largest possible serves with every meal! In the end I had to throw half of it out, even after giving some to Yankaninna and Mt Serle.

The job was still very enjoyable in itself and we were having a fair bit of fun in between work. One of the blokes was fairly superstitious and a bit gullible. I had been telling him how *Mulga monkeys* had been seen in this area, and that they were potentially dangerous. One dark night I went out to the boiler and burned both ends of a 1.3 centimetre thick mulga stick. When both ends were well and truly glowing, I took the 30 centimetre long stick outside and placed it in the fork of a nearby mulga. The light breeze kept them smouldering. The effect from the verandah was of the glowing red eyes of … ….. a *mulga monkey* maybe?

I went into the hut and a few minutes later Haggis looked out the window (he was in on it) and yelled "Hey, come and have a look at this." Bob (the gullible one) said "what the bloody hell is it?" "Probably a bull mulga monkey" I replied. Bob dragged his swag in with Haggis and I, refusing to stay on the verandah. Before I went to bed I made a few scratch marks on the mulga with an old bale hook and *constructed* a set of unusual tracks, making away from the tree. That night as Bob snored the night away, I thought, there is always a price to pay!

Then one night, came a moment of truth. We had moved north to the remote Mount Freeling Station, a large run incorporating the magnificent Freeling Heights, on the northern end of the Flinders Ranges. We were camped in a very rudimentary corrugated iron one roomed hut, without a fridge or stove, showers, etc. More or less camped out but with a roof over our heads.

This was some of the most wild and remote regions of the Flinders, and it was very enjoyable as well as challenging, working there. The drop off and pick up took longer because of the inaccessible terrain. One of the blokes had come off his bike, resulting in a suspected fractured leg. He had been taken out and in addition to my own work I was also taking samples on bike and foot, in effect, working for two bosses (McPhar Geophysics and Mt Rose Mines). My job was nearly finished, although the crew were going to be spending another week or so in the area, catering for themselves.

Early on a Sunday morning I was returning from Leigh Creek flicks with Patti. She had been quiet for a while, and I sensed there was something on her mind. The she said "Rex, how old are you?" "Only twenty six", I replied. I knew Patti was just eighteen, so there was nearly eight years difference. The silence lasted almost from one grid on the road to the next. I knew my answer had had an impact and not a good one. Everything was still friendly but the relationship was somehow different. Before I left we made arrangements to meet in Adelaide that summer when Patti's family came down on holidays.

That we did, going to the beach a few times and out to dinner in the city, but nothing too serious. Then, Patti went back to Mount Serle, and I went out to the Nullarbor in Western Australia, contract fencing. I was in a bad way. I wrote letters that were not answered, and resorted to poetry. Finally, in desperation I spent a fortune at a florist, asking them to send an arrangement of *forget me nots*. I don't know if that's what she received, but she would have got the message.

Finally, I gave up… … … …..temporarily. I knew that Patti had gone to Adelaide to Business College. Whenever I was able to (not often) I called into Mt Serle, and actually retired my old kelpie bitch (Tibun) there. It was difficult for my parents at McLaren Vale to look after her while I was working, and she was better off on the station getting a bit of sheep work in the yards. It also gave me an excuse to call in and see how she was getting on (and how Patti was getting on!)

So she was out of sight, but not out of mind. I took other girls out in between my bush trips, but no serious relationships.

Then, on one rainy Saturday night, I was in a phone box in Hindley Street. I had rung a couple of girls who couldn't or wouldn't go out. I thought, bugger it – I'll give Patti a ring. I did so, and after what I thought was a reasonable reception, I said "I don't suppose you'd want to go out tonight?" "Actually, I would", she replied, and I bloody near fell out of the phone box! We had a good night, and to cut a long story shorter, were engaged in six months.

I was never paid for my work with the Mount Rose Mining company, as they went broke. That was the down side of that job.

However, I did gain a wife!

5
THE TRUCK SAGA

Buying trucks is a serious business, especially second hand ones. I have owned a few camel trucks and by and large have had a pretty good run, however that good run came to an end in May 2006. I had just finished a 13 day camel trek around part of a very spectacular and remote section of the Great Australian Bight, in South Australia. I did it in conjunction with a mate of mine (Spitta), using several of his camels. He and his wife Trina and children (Cody and Cedar) live in an extraordinary house in the Mallee and sand dunes near Port Sinclair. It is a two storied hexagonal shape built from Hebel bricks. It rises out of the scrub in a very dramatic manner, yet seems to fit in comfortably with the environment. Solar power, with everything recycled that is recyclable. Spitta leases a large tract of land running west along the coast, running a few camels here. This was our starting point and finishing point, it had been a good trip despite a fair bit of light rain activity. We had loaded my seven camels on to my old ex army Blitz camel truck and my other cameleer (Ryan) and I had set off, me following the camel truck in my Oka 4WD. We only travelled three kilometres, when I saw the Blitz roll to a silent stop. Ryan said there had been a tapping noise before the engine died. While this was happening, Spitta was sitting down in the kitchen with Trina, congratulating himself on the quick loading. It is always a relief to get camels on the road after loading. No matter how many times you do it, there is always scope for problems. He heard me returning in the Oka, and didn't like the sound of that, and my news confirmed his thoughts. The long and short of it, after an inspection by a good local mechanic, was that the conrod had tried to *peck* its way out of the block! Very bad diagnosis. I had intended buying another truck that year, but at leisure. All of a sudden urgency was very much the order of the day. Spitta is a good mate and a very generous bloke. He said I could leave my camels with him for as long as was needed, but I knew it was putting him and his resources under a lot of pressure. We towed the truck load of camels, with the Oka, back up Spitta's track and unloaded them, one of the shortest trips ever.

I then drove back to Port Augusta, picked up Bill Oliver (who had already left to help with the transfer) and drove to a farm out the back of Orroroo to drop Ryan at his vehicle. We camped there the night, Bill and I driving home the next morning. I was driving down to Adelaide with Bill, when I received a call from Matt Reilly at Burra. He knew I was after a truck, and told me about a 1989 Acco International, with a 6 metre tray, that was available for sale at Port Adelaide. The seller had $15,000 on it which was a maximum figure for the model, but Matt had been assured it was in good condition, and sounded like it could suit my purposes. Matt knew of the bloke, who was a carrier at Port Adelaide. I thanked him and said I would look at it. I had arranged to inspect another similar vehicle, a 1980 Acco Inter. Bill and I did so. The cab was a bit rough but the truck seemed in good order, with a little bit to spend. The dealer was asking $9,000.

I made the point here that under normal circumstances I would have had a *truckie* mate with me. I have had a fair bit to do with vehicles, but I'm not a mechanic. One bloke in particular couldn't accompany me for at least three days, and knowing my camels were putting pressure on Spitta, put urgency on the matter. Bill had to return home, so I rang the bloke at Port Adelaide and drove down there. He showed me a very clean looking truck. He specifically told me that he had put a 1980 cab on it, as the other had been damaged, but that it was a 1989 model. I had a good look and took it for a drive, and was pretty comfortable with it. He agreed to reduce the price to $14,000.

Now this bloke was originally from the country, and seemed o.k. to me. For better or for worse I am a handshake man, and have rarely been let down. I asked him for the registration certificate, and he said he had mislaid it, but would send it on. Fair enough I thought, little realising that if I had seen it, it would have been obvious what I was buying was a 1980 model truck. Anyway I returned the next morning with a bank cheque and paid for the truck, and drove it home. I paid a lot for the truck. More than I intended. But reasoned that I had a 1989 instead of 1980 vehicle, and shouldn't need to spend much on it for a year or two.

Next morning Patti and I and our two Jack Russell's left for Wirraminna Station near Woomera, where a young mate (Michael Wilkinson) had offered me a crate for the truck. We were only just down the road three kilometres, when we had some fuel trouble. I mucked around with it for a while without any joy, then rang Steve Beard, a mechanic up the road a bit at Taylorville. He came down and eventually got us going, but while he was under the truck, he had seen that the rear brakes had a problem. "Sort them out on our return" I said. On our way, then more fuel troubles between Morgan and Burra. Limped into Burra and David Thamm put an electric fuel pump on as a booster in the line. Got going again, but 20 kilometres out ran out of puff and returned slowly to David's garage. This time he went further, shortening the fuel pickup pipe and this seemed to cure the problem.

By this time it was 4 pm and we headed off doing 65 kilometres per hour, flat-out, the seller had assured me it would sit on 80. Eventually reaching Port Augusta and finally Wirraminna at 1am. Michael was still up having a beer or two with a couple of Jackeroos. We had several of them before rolling our swag out in front of the open fire at 2:30 am.

Next morning the crate went on without too much trouble, just a bit of cutting and shutting, I was very grateful for this crate. It wasn't quite long enough, but I had arranged for the rest of the back to be built at Penong. We had an enjoyable drive via Kingoonya, Kokatha Station, and down through my old stamping ground of Lake Everard. Truck was slow but travelling okay. Eventually, arrived at Spitta's after dark, with the motor throwing out a fair bit of diesel, mostly from loose injectors. It was five days since I had left the camels.

Over the next three days the rear of the truck was rebuilt, with the roof rack of the old Blitz and the drop board removed (by Spitta earlier), and put onto my new truck. Kevin Thomas did the welding at the work shop in

Penong, with Spitta and I off-siding. Patti stayed down with Trina, going for walks on the beach and helping with house chores. Kevin did an excellent job on the truck, and another mate of Spittas found me some rubber conveyor matting for the sides and floor of the crate. Penong is a special little town, very *tight* group of people, enjoying their status of being outside the council area. They tend to *take care of things themselves* and one way or another, I was very well looked-after in all areas. The truck was still in doubt, but I certainly had the best camel crate that I had ever had. The camels went on without too much trouble, and Patti and I headed home, a long day, arriving at 2 am. That morning we took the truck up to Steve Beards', and opened a Pandora's box. There was a large hole on top of the axle housing near the *diff,* somehow we had completed our drive without a major accident. The whole rear end plus the brakes, was a mess. Then it transpired that everything turned out to be 1980, it was a 1980 truck. In the period that we were away the registration certificate had arrived, clearly showing this. I phoned up the seller, but he really didn't want to know about it, so I said I would see him in court. I think that surprised him a bit and I wasn't going to take this lying down. I was spending big dollars on the truck, and had to hire another local truck to truck camels up to Pandi Pandi Station to start a 16 day Sturt Stoney Desert camel trek, because mine wouldn't be ready.

Later in the year Matt Reilly and I drove up to Olary to pick up a load of cooking oil (we were making our own diesel). We were on our way back in hot weather, with plenty of stops because of overheating. Finally with no warning the motor seized, north of Hallet. Matt organized a couple of mates from Burra to come up with another truck, and tow us to David Thamm's at Whitehart Motors. Matt felt really bad about this truck, having putting me on to it in the first place, but he didn't have to.

Another mate in Adelaide found me another 354 Perkins motor out of a street sweeper, which was in really good nick. It was sent up to Burra and David performed his usual excellent job in installing it. It seemed that I finally had an old but fairly honest truck. With the purchase price it had cost up to $32,000. I had decided to represent myself in court, suing the seller for $16,000 and the date was set. With his agreement, I subpoenaed Matt as a witness; we duly arrived at the Port Adelaide Magistrates Court, and went into the court room. No sign of the seller, but there was a lady sitting down in the court. I asked the magistrate who the lady was, and she replied that she was the seller's secretary. It appeared that he had to suddenly drive to Woomera on a job the night before. Very convenient, and the magistrate wasn't too happy either. So another date was set.

Some months later Matt and I once again went to Adelaide and into court, only to find that the seller wasn't there. He had told the court he was involved as a witness in an industrial case. The lady magistrate spat the dummy when she heard this, stating that, an industrial case shouldn't take precedence over a civil case. Reilly and I wouldn't know, but thought it was good for our case that the lady was annoyed.

For the third time Matt and I journeyed to Adelaide. Twenty four hours earlier I had received a call from a woman (unnamed) in Port Adelaide Magistrates courts, informing me that the trial time had been put forward by an hour and a half. Fair enough, I let Matt know. I arrived later and half an hour before the new time, met Matt at the court. We went in, waiting an hour, with nothing happening. Finally I went to the desk, and to my amazement was told that the trial had already taken place. Without my presence, at the original time. I kicked up a hell of a fuss. Staff were a bit embarrassed, but couldn't throw any light on the matter. The woman who had phoned me was away sick. Finally they told me that I could reinstate the case, but this would involve me coming down one more time. Is it any wonder people go *off the rails* when dealing with bureaucracy? So a date was fixed. For the fourth time I came down and went into the court room, where a lady magistrate was in attendance. She seemed to take a special interest in me, coming right out and implying that I had a rough trot. She said that she could make a judgment there and then, but said that it would look better if the other party, the seller, was present. She encouraged me to get more witnesses. I went back home and told Steve Beard he had better have a day in court. Like Matt Reilly, he was a very credible witness, and has been involved in the saga from the beginning.

The day arrived for me and for the fifth time, I entered the court room. This time the seller was present, shuffling through a great wad of papers, can't imagine what they would have been. The case got going with the same lady magistrate officiating. As it progressed I actually started enjoying myself. I had nothing to lose and everything to gain. The seller was made to look pretty stupid on some occasions. I found Reilly's effort on the stand very entertaining. A very spirited performance, telling the court that this was not the way transactions were carried out in the bush, and when questioned on his testimony, got quite indignant, stating that he was also a handshake man. Went down well.

Steve Beard did well, even under some difficult questions from the seller, and *blind Freddy* could tell that his evidence was squeaky clean. The magistrate summed up and finally came down in our favour, awarding a sum of $7000. This was the difference in value of a 1980 and 1989 Acco International. I felt sure that she would like to award more, I was still over $10,000 out of pocket. Unfortunately the *Buyer Beware* factor applied no matter what circumstances. It was my problem. The magistrate then asked the seller if he envisaged a problem in paying, she had given him three weeks to pay. He mumbled on about not being happy with the principal of it, so the magistrate told him, he had better make it 11 days to pay! That shut him up! I had a technical win but hadn't been awarded any costs.

After 11 days had passed, no money had been paid, surprise! surprise! so the matter was put into the hands of the sheriff. After some weeks we found out that the seller had changed his address 11 months ago. So once again they informed me that I would have to come to Adelaide to take out a warrant of sale, meaning that the sheriff would call on our man and ascertain whether he could sell anything of his possessions, not under his company name. But the onus was on me to come up with his new address. Unbelievable! I'm a safari operator, not a bloody private detective. Anyway I contacted one of my contract cameleers, Steve Tuckwell who, by various means, was able to come up with the current address.

I eventually engaged a *sympathetic lawyer* in Adelaide to exert maximum pressure on the *seller*. His advice to me was not to hold out for $7,000. It would mean going back to court, with still no guarantee of getting it, and I had just about enough of courtrooms. So we hit the seller with an order (Layman's language) for $5,000 up front, or we would go through the whole procedure which would have meant jail for him if he didn't *cough up*. The *seller* tried it on for $3,000, but we held out and finally scored the $5,000. Still just closing the gate on a moral victory, as I was way out of pocket, but it might make the *seller* think twice about trying it on with anyone else. You live in hope.

6
FOUR WHEEL DRIVE VEHICLES I HAVE OWNED

In years gone by, in the bush, blokes (in particular) would discuss horses. These days it is mostly four wheel drives that forms the main topic of conversation when the subject of getting round the bush comes up.

I have been operating outback safaris for forty four years, and during that time have had a fair variety of vehicles. Here are a few thoughts on my experience with different makes of four wheel drives.

I will make mention here of my lifelong devotion to Peugeot cars, but I covered that in *Go with the Flow* in a chapter entitled *My Love Affair with Peugeots*.

During my six years on sheep stations before getting into the safari business I had experience with a variety of four wheel drives.

In 1960 most station managers drove around in a Holden ute, and an experienced competent bush driver could get a ute places where a novice in a 4WD wouldn't get. In that year there wasn't a 4WD on Lilydale station, where I was jackarooing.

Then in 1961 I went to Lake Everard (In the NW of South Australia) as a Jackeroo, and Land Rovers were the only make to be used, all long wheel base ute bodies.

In late 1962 the company send me over to Rawlinna, a huge developing station on the west side of the Nullarbor Plain, in Western Australia.

Here we had one CJ6 Jeep, a commercial model of the army Jeep. In my opinion not as robust and reliable as the army Jeep. Later that year I sold my FB Holden ute and became the proud owner of an army jeep (Willy's). It was my pride and joy. I bought it during my Christmas break back home in SA, and in the New Year drove it back to Western Australia. It's a long way in a jeep, and by the time I got to Eucla I began to think there just might be something in the flat Earth theory! The motor had done a lot of work, and in the end I had to get the pistons coiferised to save a major engine overhaul. Anyway I enjoyed that vehicle.

A mate Graham Campbell was contract fencing at the time, and he had an Austin Champ (ex British Army). That was quite an impressive vehicle. It had a Rolls Royce motor with five forward and five reverse gears. Designed to drive under water, everything was well sealed with a snorkel attachment down the side. Pretty heavy on the juice, but an exciting vehicle.

A local dogger and prospector also had one, as well as a British Army Humber that he used to swear by. It had a very rounded cab.

When I was back in South Australia overseeing on Bimbowrie Station (north of Olary) my vehicle was an American International Scout. This was a very different 4WD, more like a car to drive. Very good petrol motor, but we had a lot of trouble with gear boxes. Didn't like heavy loads either. There was also a CJ6 Jeep on the place.

When I began operating safaris my first vehicle was a long wheel base Land Rover station wagon. These were actually a very suitable vehicle for our operations. A four cylinder petrol motor they were reasonably economical by the days standard. We had a full length roof rack, and because we were always overloaded, had an extra leaf in the rear springs. We carried six all up with big loading in the rear (food, grog, etc) with swags and personal bags filling the roof rack.

One good thing about Land Rover wagons was their *square* build. It meant lots of extra loading space. With aluminium bodies, even with our big top loads, they were pretty stable if driven appropriately. We used to still break rear springs, usually the top leaf just to the front or rear of the axle housing. So we always carried *spring clamps* consisting of a short length of spring and two U clamps. Always used to get me home without having to change a spring (a bastard of a job).

However, there always seemed to be some sort of minor problem with Land Rovers, so I had something of a love/hate relationship. One thing though, there are few vehicles even today that could outperform those old Land Rovers in the sand.

Another good feature they did have (way before air-conditioning came in) was the two large front air vents. On the hottest day they weren't too bad. You had the large roof load, and with your vents open a big flow of air coming through, even though it wasn't always cool. In addition, driving through heavy bull dust, the vehicle was completely pressurised with no dust coming in.

For a few years I greatly admired the heavy (2 ton) 4WD Internationals – the AB120, C-1300 and D1310. I carried Len Beadell on a couple of trips and he often mentioned they were used earlier by various government departments, and he was impressed by them.

One summer I was looking after Nullarbor Station for a mate, the late Murray Thomas, and one day three vehicles arrived from the North. They were bush surveyors, and the lead vehicle was a grey AB120 International. It really made my day.

The next year we did the first tourist crossing of the Simpson Desert and John Gibson (the surveyor) bought the International as our main stores carrier. It performed exceptionally well, including crossing the flooding Eyre Creek with water half way up its doors.

The very next year I sold my Land Rover and became the proud owner of an AB120 4X4 International van. I had a body builder put another side door and extra windows in. It had barn doors and carried 9 passengers all up. There was a full length roof rack, with a reasonable loading space in the rear.

I had this vehicle for a couple of years, before eventually selling it and buying an ex DCA (Department of Civil Aviation) C-1300 International from Darwin, with only 5,800 miles on the clock. This turned out to be the best safari vehicle I have had to date. It did a consistent 5.5 kilometres to the litre (12 miles per gallon), and the excellent International motor burnt hardly a drop of oil. It was a single cab, but I had a second cab built on (called the *fish tank*). This had sliding windows/doors and the occupants had to look through the rear window of the front cab, so we had a PA system to enable them to communicate with the front passengers. A six seater.

The large rear loading area was enclosed with heavy duty khaki canvas, and had a roof rack on top. Above the *fish tank* was a canvas zippered *hatch* that could be opened for wildlife filming, or shooting on occasions. Travelling along it was often used as a *sun roof* with the hatch open, until the Doberman bitch I used to carry on the front roof rack *let go* one day, and wiped out the three occupants of the fish tank!

This vehicle did annual trips to Cape York, and many desert crossings, fitted with the original Michelin Sahara tyres (another great invention of the time).

While I still ran this C-1300, I bought a new D1310, with a factory fitted rear cab. Same canvas back, but a full length roof rack. This was a good vehicle, but somehow I never valued it as much as the C-1300, which ended up as a fire truck on my farm on the west end of Kangaroo Island.

After seven or eight years with the Internationals, I bought a low mileage Toyota 60 series wagon, which was quite a good vehicle mechanically, but you couldn't get the amount of gear in that the Land Rover could handle, in the back and on top. Also, the front middle seat wasn't a real option like the Land Rovers, with more possibility of sexual harassment charges. Soon after I purchased a very clean FJ45 Troop Carrier (Toyota).

This proved a much better safari vehicle than the wagon which I also kept. I worked this combination for a number of years, before selling them and buying a new Toyota Troop Carrier with a door cut in the near side. The middle seat carried two, with a car fridge sitting near the near side seat, with a bench seat in the rear, making it a seven seater. The down side was that it had very little loading area in the rear, and as I try and avoid towing trailers (the thirteenth commandment reads – *Thou shall not tow a trailer in the desert*) I needed to look at another vehicle as well. What I came up with proved very successful for a number of years.

For some time I had been interested in the ex-Army International Acco 4WD trucks. This was the new generation *Blitz*, replacing the old World War II Chev and Ford Blitzes, real icons but comfort was their last priority.

There was a sale at Sunshine in outer Melbourne, and myself and Evan Graske went over on the Melbourne Express to attend. There was a Red ex-Army fire vehicle that was just cab/chassis with only 8000 kilometres on the clock. I couldn't believe it was up for auction and I was desperate to get it. There were only a couple of other bidders and they didn't seem all that keen, and I couldn't believe my luck when it was knocked down for $7,500. We left soon after, and it drove like the new vehicle it almost was. I was delighted, and a week later we found out from a contact of Evan's that it was not supposed to have been auctioned! An army *stuff up*, but much to our advantage.

It was an enjoyable drive back across the border and I spent a bit of time standing on the passenger seat and sticking my head out of the round roof hatch like *Colonel Nut*.

At one place we came across some road workers leaning on their shovels, and I abused them for letting the country down. A few hundred metres on the motor started cutting out, and I thought the mob might descend on us with their shovels, but it was only Evan having a bit of fun running with the choke out!

Soon after I arrived home at McLaren Flat, *Duff* Sigston began fitting it out. This consisted of building a back on it. It had a rear door in the centre with open window space down each side. From shoulder height (when seated), it had heavy duty khaki canvas up and over a curved steel runner on the roof. This was designed to roll right up giving passengers exceptional viewing. There were gaps cut into the canvas so that when rolled down Perspex windows could be inserted. Very versatile.

On the steel roof we built a massive pack rack with a marine ply floor. It was big enough to land an Iroquois Helicopter, and to this day I don't know how the Department passed it.

There was a smaller front roof rack (still large) over the cab, and mounted above this was a frame with two Morris 1000 bucket seats mounted on it. These were taken off during annual inspections. I also used them on the Internationals. They had seat belts, and were ideal for filming wildlife, both when stationary and moving. Never legal but we got away with it. People loved them, and I drove accordingly when people were in them. The only real drama we had law wise was once when I drove into Eucla from a bit of cross country Nullarbor travelling, the local cop nearly swallowed his hat! He couldn't believe it (there were people in them), and I had to dismantle them on the spot, and promise never to use them again! He went right off, telling me I was very irresponsible, but afterwards, bowing to intense public pressure, we put them back up there. Those days, people were permitted to be responsible for their own actions, unlike the present day. The rampant creed of occupational, health and safety rules supreme.

This was a very successful vehicle that I kept for twelve years, operating in partnership with the Troop carrier. We put a decent 354T Perkins motor in and it used to do a consistent 5.5 kilometres to the litre (12 miles per gallon) which wasn't too bad. Very comfortable to ride in, and would cruise at 85 to 90 km/hr.

In the rear I had a large tucker/gear box running almost the full length of the back with a padded top. There were single speed boat seats down the sides with a bench seat across the back, carrying 13 passengers and it had a PA system from the front. It had the standard massive army winch on the front that could pull both front and rear, and I had a couple of 3.65 metres 25 centimetre x 5 centimetre bog boards inserted under the back of the tray. This vehicle operated all over the outback, with the exception of a Simpson Desert crossing.

One year we took it right up to Cape York which was definitely a *one off*. Did a clutch at Lakefield which held us up for a couple of days. That was a memorable trip.

Had a funny one at Wyndham one Kimberley trip. We were pulled up, when an Australian Pacific tourist coach arrived and stopped nearby. Our sides were all rolled up for the tropical travel. A number of coach passengers came over to the Blitz, taking photos and talking to some of my people. They were clearly envious, and my people gave them some of my brochures. Next minute the Australian Pacific Coach Captain came hurrying over clad immaculately in his smart uniform. He obviously didn't like the *cross pollination*, and said to some of my people "Look, you don't have to travel like that these days – you can have air conditioning". He was horrified by the look of the *Blitz* with the open sides, and the whole jizz of it, to use an ornithological term. But it all fell on deaf ears, and he walked off in disgust.

It wasn't the sort of vehicle you wanted to get bogged. On one memorable occasion up on the Gulf of Carpentaria I bogged it badly. Luckily we were driving in to a three day base camp, and it took us a fair bit of that time to dig it out.

Around this time I picked up an old series ute body Land Rover to use up at the camel camp on Merna Mora Station in the Flinders Ranges. I was driving it up there one night, and was half way around the Gawler Bypass when the engine seized. I flagged a bloke down and he towed me around to his place, where I rolled my swag out on his shed floor. Eventually it was repaired and used up at the camp for a couple of years. I liked the look of those old series models.

When Range Rovers appeared on the market they created quite a stir. Here at last, the advertising said, was a serious 4WD with the comfort of a European sedan, with constant four wheel drive. At the time Champion Motors in Adelaide had the agency. I did a deal with them when we bought out a combined ad for them and my business (which at that time was called *Transcontinental Safaris*).

It was 1974 and I paid a slightly discounted price of $8,000. It was quite an exciting vehicle to drive with the very smooth powerful V8 motor.

Although a five seater, I had a small centre seat installed in the middle, matching the upholstery, to try and boost my carrying capacity but it was never really satisfactory. There was a roof rack, but the carrying space was way less than a Toyota or Land Rover wagon.

The vision was good with big windows front and sides, but without the air conditioning it was a real *glass house* in warm weather. The lack of three or four doors was not popular for rear passengers (since remedied with four door models)

The early models had the fuel pump down low by the fuel tanks, and this caused real problems travelling through water (a water proofing problem since remedied). Very good in sand, but on a number of occasions while cross country driving, particularly through spinifex, fires would start due to vegetable matter jammed under the sump guard that I had fitted.

Carrying loads on the top (heavy ones like we had to) cause these vehicles to be more potentially dangerous than most others. On one occasion coming down the lower Tanami track, following rain, one of my drivers tipped it over, through no real fault of his own. It had wide sand tyres fitted. I was in front driving my C-1300 International, and went through a sticky patch that caused my rear end to *wag*, just a little. When the Range Rover went through it got into a slide, and when it came up against the wind row, rolled on to its side and slid along about twenty metres before hitting a mulga. Caused by the wide tyres, with tread well down and substantial top load. No one seriously hurt, but the vehicle was badly damaged.

The insurance decided not to write it off, so it was repaired, and at two years old I sold it for $8,000, the same price I paid for it. So they kept their value very well. They are no doubt a good vehicle for a couple or family that wants to do long distance driving, but not much good for a safari vehicle or serious 'bush bashing'.

I must have had a rush of blood to the head, because I lashed out and bought a new 4WD International Scout station wagon. It looked very impressive painted light green and white. Wasn't impressed for too long. It had the usual very good International motor, was relatively comfortable with a good loading area – the loading area was good provided you carried a mob of empty cardboard cartons! The suspension was hopeless, and it would bottom out with the lightest of loads. Totally useless for safari work.

I took it to Adelaide and traded it on an early 1980's Toyota Troop Carrier, which was a good reliable vehicle for a number of years.

There's no doubt about Toyotas, they are a good vehicle, and continue to develop whereas Land Rovers rested on their laurels and stayed the same for years. It was often joked that the British developed Land Rover without any input from *the colonies,* telling us what we had to have. Whereas, the japs came along, cap in hand, and asked us what we wanted in a 4WD vehicle, and went and manufactured it. Which is why Toyotas totally routed Land Rovers in the 4WD stakes, in Australia and probably around the world.

For a couple of years I owned a 3 speed Toyota station wagon. I bought it more for novelty value than anything else, and because I liked the look of it. I didn't use it much on the trips, and eventually (reluctantly) sold it for a profit.

My next effort was a result of a Blinman mate of mine called Irving Cains. He is a devoted Land Rover man (a true *affictionado*) and he had a 101 Forward control Land Rover. These were purchased by the Australian army from the British army to tow the British Rapier missile systems. This was another one of my bad errors of judgement, although this takes away nothing form the effectiveness of the vehicle. They were more of a *4x4 tractor* than anything else. Long travel springs, a Range Rover motor, which was good. A very small *racing* steering wheel, it was a go places vehicle. Great torque, it could almost climb a vertical wall (almost!)

For a one person vehicle for some serious 4WD work it was very good. But no good to me. For a start it was very noisy (all canvas cab) and bad fumes. Sharp edges everywhere which gave it one out of ten for comfort, although the long travel springs meant it rode well over corrugation and gutters. People didn't like riding in it, and who could blame them. So I eventually sold it, reluctantly, because I had a soft spot for it.

And now for what will possibly be my final *work vehicle,* the Oka.

Okas came about in the late 1980's as a result of a few knowledgeable 4WD men, some of which were involved in the mining industry, getting together. The chief light *workhorse* in the mining industry was the Toyota Land Cruiser, and it was stated that, on the average, one would last under the most extreme mining conditions, probably with a number of drivers, around nine months and then scrapped. When they finally developed the Oka, they reckoned it would last around fourteen months before refurbishing for around $25,000. That assessment was never really substantiated. Even though a very effective performer under the most extreme conditions, high maintenance costs and a high purchase price, plus alleged poor customer service proved them unsuitable. Instead they gained a ready acceptance in the tourist industry and various government departments including the police in some states, fire services, etc. They were also exported overseas for use in some countries military forces.

Built in modules they could be shipped overseas for reassembly.

Right from the start the Oka Motor Company (as it was initially called) received minimal help from the government.

Without going into great detail, they bought out three models, all of very similar appearance, the first two with big bore turbo charged four cylinder Perkins diesel motors. A bit under powered in some circumstances, but with exceptional torque.

Very good suspension with long travel springs, (the idea probably borrowed from 101 Land Rovers) and the option of double shock absorbers all round. Empty or loaded, this gives a great ride over rough terrain, particularly corrugations – almost a *hover craft* ride with the tyres down a bit. Their high clearance coupled with the excellent torque gives impressive rugged hill climbing ability. There are two settings on the rear springs for light or heavy loading, but mine are always on the high setting.

One of the few medium size vehicles to have the ROPS (Roll Over Protection System) rating, which is a very good feature. They are also designed to drive underwater up to around driver waist height. You probably wouldn't want to make a habit of that, but it's comforting to know you have the option.

They are certainly not perfect, but all in all there is no other vehicle on the market that can adequately do the work that I require a vehicle to do.

I have had 9 seater multicabs only. (Any body style can be swapped in under a day). These give me a massive loading area in the canvas covered rear or on the large roof rack. Another feature I might mention is that they have the same track as a 'conventional 4 x 4', a big plus when driving on two wheel tracks.

To the ongoing despair of Oka owners, the company seems to stagger from one crisis to the next, but even with large time lapses between productions, they are still hanging in there. As I write this, production is stalled once again after recently bringing out a new model with a four cylinder Cummins diesel (185hp compared to 110hp in the Perkins) and an optional manual or automatic transmission. There are a number of Okas around with over one million kilometres on the clock, and still going strong, and considering their price they would want to last a lifetime. They make an excellent *camper* as many can attest.

I sold my first Oka (1995 model LT) in 2011, because at the time the relevant department would not ok a multicab operating as a *hire-fare-reward* vehicle if it was over 15 years old or with more than 400,000 km on the clock. Mine came under that category, and so to keep operating my business I was forced to sell it. Fortunately I was able to get hold of the last LT model off the assembly line that was owned by the previous General Manager of the company. He had indulged himself. It was a multicab with six doors, and some of the features of the new models, including the transfer case. With only 130,000 kilometres on the speedo it was a very good proposition for me. Luckily Okas hold their resale value well.

A few 'Oka incidents' of interest.

A mate of mine (Graham Campbell) was the Federal member for Kalgoorlie for twenty years. His was the largest electorate in the world, and he was given an Oka as his work vehicle (at his request). He was visiting Woolleen Station in the Murchison, and had Rosemary, his secretary, with him.

At the time the Gascoyne River was in flood, with vehicles held up each side at the Woolleen crossing. Graham left the homestead and drove down to the river to have a look. It was after dark. He though the Oka was capable of crossing. Here was a man who rarely knew fear, and either Rosemary was the same, or didn't have any option, because Graham decided to give it a go such was his confidence in the vehicle. What he didn't know, was that the concrete causeway had a curve in it, and this was what brought him undone.

In low range bottom he moved out into the water, with the eyes of the many stranded people fixed on him. It was about fifty metres across. He was going ok until his right hand front wheel ran off the side of the cause way. Too late to reverse, and thinking he would roll if he continued on with a wheel off, or if he tried to climb back on – he turned the Oka hard on the right hand and headed off down the river!

The water was up to the top of the doors. The Oka aircleaner is on the driver side around the level of the driver's head. He travelled for about thirty metres when he entered a deep hole and the Oka was actually floating! He was only around thirty metres from the other bank. Graham and Rosemary crawled out of the windows and sat on the roof. Water poured through the open windows, until the level was up to the top of the doors. Graham took his coat off (he always wore a suit) plus shoes, and swam to the other bank where he was met by some amazed aboriginals who worked for the shire.

They headed off for a bit, returning with a large loader and cable. Graham swam back out with the cable, dived under the front of the Oka and attached the cable. The Oka was then towed out of the river and up on to the bank. (Before he swam for the bank, the motor was still running, and he had to turn it off).

The vehicle went to the Oka Motor Company in Perth on a low loader where it had the necessary work carried out to render it operative again. No real damage, although due to inadequate work behind the dashboard, Graham had corrosion problems in the wiring later on.

All in all though it wasn't a bad add for Oka, and if they had a decent advertising division (which they don't) they could have extracted a lot of mileage out of the event.

Another mate Peter Young, of Alltrac 4WD in Adelaide, is a very experienced four wheel driver, and has owned an Oka, that he converted into an excellent camper. For a number of years he was the SA agent for Okas, but he's given it up due to the unreliability of supply, and the ongoing costs of maintaining the agency. However he still maintains a number of local Okas including mine.

The LT series had an unsuitable Rockwell transfer case which was not designed for the road speed of the vehicle. It required a lot of maintenance. Peter took it out and with a clever bit of engineering installed a GQ Nissan transfer case and running gear.

It is generally accepted that the GQ Nissan Patrols have one of the strongest drive trains around. It was very successful in all areas.

Robin Wade, another Oka expert operates *Oka Kalgoorlie* based at Coolgardie in WA. He has a recovery vehicle, a specially fitted out Oka. The local Gold Fields police call on him for the more difficult recovery jobs in the local area.

For a number of years Robin has supplied Okas and trained local drivers for specialised operations in New Guinea. There are several upmarket tourist lodges operated by Trans New Guinea Tours in the New Guinea highlands that use Okas exclusively. Their clearance, weight, torque and Perkins engines allow them to operate to altitudes in excess of 2400 metres. No other vehicle trialled has been able to do this successfully.

These vehicles rarely get out of low range second, and regularly cross rough fast running creeks and climb steep grades, surely one of the most extreme tests for any vehicle.

Why the name *Oka*? Well they originally waited to call it an *Ocker* (after the *Aussie ocker*, but that name was already registered. So they just settled on *Oka*.

The only Australian made four wheel drive occupies a niche that is unlikely to be challenged for years to come.

I did say that the Oka would possibly be my last work vehicle. Well, that could be, but depending on how much longer I operate, there's a more than even chance I could end up with another Toyota – the FJ Cruiser. Good solid features based on the successful Prado. You either strongly like or dislike their appearance, and I like it. Will see what happens.

That's probably enough about four wheel drives for many readers, but they have been (and still are) a big part of my life.

7
THE GREAT DESERT RIVERS

COOPER AND WARBURTON 2009-11

The year 2009 was the beginning of a three year bonanza for the Cooper and Warburton rivers. Their normal status of rivers of sand west of the Birdsville Track underwent the usual magical transformation as the *Queensland water* made its way to Lake Eyre. This time though it was not the one-off yearly run, or maybe two, but an incredible three years of running water into Lake Eyre – at least, for the Warburton.

During this period I did something like thirty desert boat safaris (covering approximately eight thousand kilometres in boats), the great majority on the Cooper, Warburton and Kallakoopah systems. This chapter deals with highlights and various incidents that occurred during these three years.

It began with a contract with channel seven who were doing a documentary on Lake Eyre. It was for their *Sunday Night* program, and covered mainly the Lake Eyre Yacht Club, my operation on the rivers, and the Australian Wildlife Conservancy's (AWC) activities at the recently purchased Kalamurina Station.

Prior to AWC buying Kalamurina, I had enjoyed a very good relationship with the previous owners, beginning with Jim Dunn back in 1974, when we first navigated the Warburton and crossed Lake Eyre. The Australian Wildlife Conservancy was a relatively new private conservation group, doing what John and Prue Warmsley (and myself in a small way) (see 'A Wildlife Experiment' in *Ten Thousand Campfires*) had pioneered back in the mid 1970's. They had a number of properties in Western Australia, and when Earth Sanctuaries went bankrupt, they purchased most of their successful properties.

It was a good result, and AWC and other private concerns such as Bush Heritage are doing what *National Parks and Wildlife* have failed to do – save our wildlife. I knew, and still do, many people working in AWC who are very professional and dedicated to saving our wildlife. Early in the year, I contacted AWC to formalize my operations on the Warburton, and met with some resistance from one of the principals. I suggested that they could make me their *preferred operator*, and for a while it looked like this might happen as I am the only commercial operator travelling these rivers. I had suggested to them that some of their shareholders may like to participate in the world class experience that running the floodwaters to Lake Eyre, undoubtedly is. After several conversations with this person, I found it impossible to contact him by any means, and I was passed on to his 2IC who was a reasonable person. I was given permission to operate, with road access into Kalamurina, with a set of conditions. These were reasonable enough, and a couple of trips were operated. Then, on one occasion I called into their shareholders camp (where I was supposed to avoid) in order to make an important call on their satellite phone (mine was playing up). I did this, but I was later informed that the original *principal*', who was apparently at the camp on this occasion – was *incensed*' that I had called in. It seemed like the old outback traditions were no longer relevant. Soon after, I was informed that my access had been withdrawn.

I wrote a letter to the AWC Boss with a copy to all of the directors, and after some time I had an answer from the Boss to say that I had violated my conditions (they would never be explicit about this) and that I was "banned from all AWC properties throughout Australia for one year". Pretty pathetic really. I wrote back, and said that I would continue to operate down the Warburton River, even though I was banned from travelling through Kalamurina to get access to the river. I made the point that rivers belong to all Australians. I continue to operate down the river, but always felt very unhappy with my treatment. I had earlier been a good friend to AWC, and believed in what they were doing. I also believe that if my original discussions had been with someone other than the particular 'principal', the result would have been a mutually favourable arrangement. Instead of that I am classed as an *outlaw*.

Wildlife highlights happen virtually every day in some shape or another. Wedge tailed eagles are regularly seen, their bulky nest seen in mostly Coolibahs. One exception found on one of our bush walks away from the river (Cooper) was where a four metre high Cooba (*Acacia stenophylla*) had its top *flattened,* and a nest constructed on the very top of the tree. I was able to sit on Len Cooper's shoulders and photograph the young eaglets sitting among the carcasses of dead rabbits, and sleepy lizards (Shinglebacks).

Still on Wedge tails, we were travelling down the Warburton, when a Nankeen Night Heron was seen flying frantically towards the boat a hundred metres away and only a metre or so above the water. Behind it some twenty metres was a Wedge tailed eagle, slashing the air with powerful wing beats. The heron was throwing itself from side to side. Just before that, one of the rear boat parties had seen the eagle *stoop* on the heron, but miss it.

Then, as the birds came within fifty metres of my boat another eagle joined the chase. Suddenly the heron veered right into some lignum, and disappeared. Probably a good move. The eagles flew out to a dead Coolibah and perched, no doubt needing to *recharge their batteries* for a while.

In the latter part of 2009, such was the demand, that I had two new 4.3 metre heavy duty punts made, with most trips having four boats, which meant (with boaties) an all up party of sixteen. That worked well – any more would have devalued the experience. Jason Hart (HMF Boats) in Waikerie was making excellent boats, and he also built me two heavy duty trailers.

In 2010, the Cooper finally crossed the Birdsville track half way through the year. It was expected much earlier, and the reason for its late arrival was finally revealed. Such was the volume of plant growth that had built up since the drought had broken, it appeared to slow down the massive volume of water that was making its way down from Innamincka. Another impediment was a causeway across the main channel of the Cooper holding back around 120 kilometres of water

The huge Lake Hope had filled, and the Cooper cut a partly new channel out of the lake on its way down to the Birdsville track. The interesting thing was that instead of the usual off-white coloured water, the water was greenish and almost clear. It seemed that the massive growth and bulk of herbage and other vegetation from the previous year, had filtered the water.

I had Cooper/Lake Eyre trips fully booked, but because the Cooper was taking so long to get to Lake Eyre, I decided to try and get as far as possible upstream from the ferry at the Birdsville track. I had tried in 1990, only to run out of water, so I began without huge expectations.

The first day I made about fifty river kilometres, and couldn't believe it. The navigation was far from easy with many lakes and channels, and much of the time we were on river flats, with a bit of retracing our tracks when we ran out of water. It is a totally different river than that below the *swamp* on the Birdsville track. For a start there is always Coolibahs, although nowhere *wall to wall* on the banks. This means more wildlife, and with the country green and plenty of wild flowers, it wasn't hard to take.

After three days or so we passed Lake Hope and kept going for another couple of days to Waukatanna waterhole. Could have gone further, but had to allow time to get back down the river to the ferry, where we started.

It was the day of my mate Bill Oliver's funeral, and we carried our lunch bags and billy's of water up on to a huge white sand dune. It was a scene of great beauty. We were almost surrounded by water, birds were calling, and it was a beautiful sunny day. We had a minute's silence for Bill, and hope he was tuned in. He had done countless trips with me over the years, many in boats.

Just before pulling out from the sandhill we inspected the extraordinary nest of a Pink eared Duck – a mass of down with the eggs deposited in the middle. This one was in a low shrub inches from the water, but I have seen others in hollows of Coolibahs. This duck is unique to Australia. One of the smallest, the male has a pink spot behind the ear, hard to spot unless you are close, or with good binoculars. Dark barring on the front, with a broad white tail band. The feature that fascinates many ornithologists is the filter on the end of the bill, used when feeding on minute plant matter.

They breed (often in their thousands) when floodwaters run over the banks of the channels, creating ideal conditions. During the long drought, this was pretty well non-existent, and the Pink eared duck population dropped to dangerously low levels. This three years of flooding desert rivers have been a lifesaver for the species, along with some others such as Black duck, Pelicans and Straw Necked Ibis.

If the drought had continued there was a very real possibility that we could have lost some of these species forever. The difference between this drought, and comparable ones last century, is that irrigation wasn't sucking water out of every natural resource across the country. The general public needs to be aware of the consequences of *open slather* irrigation. You live in hope.

Getting back was much easier, with the flow, and an enjoyable leisurely trip was had.

A few weeks later, the water crossed the Birdsville Track, and a week or two later was joining with the Warburton to contribute to the waters of Lake Eyre, which by now was around half full. Soon after I had four boats ready to go to the lake. I hadn't been down there since the last time it ran in 1990.

Prior to most boat safaris, people arrive at our place by car or coach. A week or so earlier, Patti had a late booking from one John Pilbrick and his wife Christine. John had mentioned that he was a *bit overweight,* and could bring his own *chair* for the boat. Patti told him it wouldn't be necessary. Don't you believe it!

When John's car pulled up, the passenger's side door opened and inside was a *man mountain*! My initial thought was "shit, we can't possibly carry him" – followed closely by the thought that if it was 1810 instead of 2010, I could have shot him!

Fortunately, we had a cancellation otherwise we definitely couldn't have carried him. I don't think that John, who was a very perceptive man, was aware of my radical thoughts.

Next day we were underway, and the following morning were pulling up at the ferry. I had a boat and trailer on the north side of the river, so unloaded the boat and took the wheels and hubs off, so that the axles could be sealed. Pushing the trailer into the river, we towed it across to the other side. By this time it was nearly dark, and with the usual good natured cooperation of the ferry men – they did an after hours run back across to bring Peter back. When John *rolled* into one of the boats (he was 170 kilograms) the very stable, heavy duty punt lurched to a forty five degree angle, so we soon had him sitting in splendid isolation in the dead centre of the boat.

By this time my (and the other *boaties,* Peter Young, Rick Moore and Graham Rivers) somewhat dark thoughts regarding Big John had been supplanted by much more charitable ones. He was a very charming person, a lawyer, with an equally large intellect and sense of humour. Despite his bulk, he really wasn't any trouble whatsoever. But I had far more pressing problems.

We had a pleasant cruise down river from the ferry and across Killamperpunna Lake.

On reaching the Birdsville Track, we boated along it half a kilometre, for a bit of fun, before turning into the very large Kopperamanna swamp. This is around 1295 square kilometres of Coolibah/Lignum/Old man Saltbush. On previous trips down the Cooper from 1974, I had no trouble (well, not too much!) getting across it, and finding the outlet where the main channel headed off towards the lake. This was without the lap full of technology that

Peter had sitting on his knees. All went well down the bore drain, and then a little detour to the monument to famous drover Bill Gwydir. But after that we were *all at sea*. Nothing seemed familiar to me, and I kept running out of flow where we should have had plenty. It was an interesting (for the party) but frustrating afternoon. Very little dry land or good water, and an hour and a half before dark I called it a day and camped on a nice little sandy island of a couple of acres. *Big John* rolled out of his boat (he had been there all day) and installed himself in his special throne-like chair in the camp. He was going well.

Next morning we headed off in what I knew was the right direction, but again kept running out of water. We were on a channel that led to the old Kilalpaninna Lutheran Mission ruins, which would have done, but kept running out of water. I later realised that I could have got through to the outlet if I had kept going, but the fear of sixteen people spending a night in the boats proved too strong a deterrent. By mid afternoon, and after seeing no campable land all day, I made the decision to turn south to try and find a camp. More shallow water trouble and bush bashing, when with only an hour or so of daylight left, we saw a sand hill in the distance. A cattle fence ran down to it, and I thought that will do us. At the fence, with only 30 centimetres of water, I decided to take off in the Zodiak inflatable (that we towed) to check the camp and take some gear in. I went about twenty metres and that too ran out of water. I was beginning to have thoughts about spending all night in the boats like we did near this location in 1974. It didn't bear thinking about.

We were very busy for the next couple of hours. Us blokes took it in turns to pull the Zodiak through the mostly deep mud for well over half a kilometre to a dry land camp. I did the first one, got some timber together and lit a fire which was a beckoning beacon for us. It took us half a dozen trips in the rubber duck to get essential gear to the camp. All this time, John and Christine had been laboriously picking their way along the barb wire fence through the mush. Full marks, but I could see he was doing it hard, and told the boys to *order* him into the duck on the last run. They didn't have to say a word as he *fell* into it, for the last few hundred metres. That was a welcome camp, but put paid to us getting to Lake Eyre this trip.

Next morning I rang Jason Dunn at Etadunna Station, and he came out and picked a couple of us up and ran us out to the ferry to get the Oka. We returned to the station and picked up a Spinning Jenny (a rotating device used to dispense a coil of wire) and a coil of high tensile wire. Returning to the boat camp, we ran wire out through the mud and water to the boats. At first we connected all boats together and tried to pull them out with the Oka. They were nearly half a kilometre away and the drag was too much, breaking the wire, so we pulled them out in pairs.

Loading up, we headed back out to the ferry, unloaded again, and headed upstream. We had a pleasant six days up and back, getting up past Lake Appadare.

Big John fell into a good routine, ably assisted by his wife Christine. He had earlier perfected his unique *roll* in and out of the boat. Most *smokos* he would stay in the boat reading, as we would often take the smoko bags with thermoses up onto a sand hill, or have a nature walk. Someone would deliver his cuppa and biscuit.

I have to say that the sound effects were interesting in the evenings when John was getting into his swag, and in the mornings with the extrication process. He proved to be such a good and popular party member, and if I had known about his *dimensions* – I would have had a special *jumbo* swag made up for him, that would have made his life a lot easier. For us blokes, because of his bulk and great attitude, it became a challenge to guide him through the potential hazards of the trip. The only actual minor problem was a bit of *collateral damage* going back in the vehicles when John broke the raised edge of Peter's front passenger seat in his Land Cruiser. The Japs, who have probably catered for the odd Sumo wrestler or two should have been able to design a bomb proof seat anyway. John had to travel in the smaller vehicles, as I would have needed a derrick to get him in and out of the Oka.

John always said he had this ability to lose weight in a short period of time, and talking to him recently he had dropped over 44 kilograms. He had been on a couple of *demanding* adventure type trips in Russia.

When John finally passes over to the other side, he will be remembered in fly fishing circles, as he designed a unique fly, that is in popular use.

Birding is a constant theme on all of these trips, as I have been a birdwatcher all of my life. When the party comprises a number of keen birders it is good for all concerned, and certainly results in more birds recorded. During one Warburton trip in 2011, half the party were birders, and it included several that were particularly good. All birdwatchers are always on the lookout for rare or difficult to get birds, and when seen, records are often sent into Birdlife Australia. Many observations sent in are unreliable or optimistic, and for this reason a panel of eminent ornithologists has been set up to review them. This often causes friction and disappointment, but it's the way it is – otherwise Night Parrots would have been off the endangered list, and Paradise Parrots would be seen on every second termite mound in south east Queensland.

We were going down river, when a couple of birders had a startling observation in the second boat. The communication on the UHF radio didn't happen as it should have, and I wasn't aware of the sighting until smoko stop. It seemed that a Northern Pintail had been sighted. This is what in ornithological terms is called a vagrant. It is a North American species, sometimes seen in South East Asia, that had only been recorded in Western Australia, near Perth, and on the NSW coast in more recent times. The male is quite a distinctive bird, with its colouring (particularly in breeding plumage) with an unusual long black tail. Unmistakable from any other Australian duck.

The sighters were very excited, and I was very frustrated because I hadn't seen it (a la Nigh Parrot in 1979!) One of these blokes (a very good birder) was particularly cautious, and didn't want to rush in to sending a report to Birdlife Australia.

On the way back upstream, despite our best efforts, no more birds were seen, and so no report was sent in. So much for some people's lack of confidence and fear of rejection. A pity, I think.

In August 2011, a tragedy occurred that made national and international news. The ABC documentary series on Lake Eyre in 2009 and 2010 had caused such interest in Australia and overseas, that it was decided to do a third documentary in 2011.

I had been involved in 2009 (with the camels in the Flinders Ranges) and in the boats on the Warburton in 2010. During those occasions I had got to know Paul Lockyer (the presenter) pretty well, and we had a very good rapport, with many telephone conversations in between. The series had proven very popular throughout the bush, as Paul Lockyer and crew (chopper pilot Gary Ticehurst and cameraman John Bean (and Ben Hawkes in 2009)) had that special knack of interviewing bush people, and were very receptive to their many problems.

Paul had rung up earlier, and arranged to meet me down at the mouth of the Cooper when I would be there with a boat party. This was the very start of the third series. Ben Hawkes (the producer) was to have been on board but at the last minute had to pull out for the first two days. Such is fate.

We were camped on a small island at the Cooper Creek inlet. Expecting the ABC chopper at about four thirty, I had a camp oven roast cooking. They had been going to camp the night with us, but arrangements had been changed. That night they were to go to Muloorina Station at the bottom of the lake, then to William Creek off the western shore next morning before returning to us for some filming.

Soon after four thirty, I heard Paul on the radio, and ten minutes later they were landing near the camp by the edge of the water.

Before continuing, I will relate another helicopter situation that occurred just twenty four hours earlier. We had a lady in our party who had a medical condition (which turned out to be pneumonia) and it was decided that she needed to be flown out.

It was arranged through the Flying Doctor that the Moomba helicopter would pick her up. After phoning 000, as is the practice these days, and speaking to someone of unidentifiable ethnic origins, who probably had a better grasp of the location of the Ganges, as compared to the Warburton. I was finally connected to the Port Augusta Royal Flying Doctor base. I obtained their direct number, as it used to be. The chopper came in with pilot and an attractive Moomba sister, and the evacuation took place. This was the first time in my forty four years of operation that an aerial evacuation had been required.

Back to our island. The chopper had landed, and Gary shut it down. All three men came to our camp, and I did the introductions. It was a very good atmosphere, with everyone in excellent humour. Paul was particularly enthusiastic, as he loved Lake Eyre, and was greatly anticipating the project.

I offered Paul and John a glass of wine, but they declined, and Gary never did anyway, when flying.

Paul did an interview with me, before we sat down to the roast of saltbush mutton. By this time, it was dark, with no moon. After the meal,

Gary went over to the chopper and carried out the usual flight checks. I make the point here that Gary Ticehurst was one of the most experienced helicopter pilots in Australia today. He was a regular in the Sydney-Hobart yacht race, and had been involved in the many rescues by helicopter during the early 90's horrific Sydney to Hobart yacht race. He was also an ex-military pilot.

Paul and John joined him on board, saying they would see us next day. The chopper took off, rising to around twenty metres, before turning and flying around the front of our camp, on our eastern side. This surprised me, because I expected it to turn south and head for Muloorina. Then I thought Gary would do a swing around our camp before heading south. However, this didn't happen. Instead, they kept flying to the north. At his stage, I wasn't concerned, just mystified. They kept heading north – we couldn't see the aircraft, but the lights were visible. They reached the other shore about half a kilometre distant, before becoming stationary in the air. They then turned, and headed due west toward Lake Eyre, at around an estimated fifty metre height. By this time I was getting concerned, as this flight pattern made no sense. The door hadn't been open for filming, and it was very dark anyway. When they had travelled around a kilometre, the helicopter again became stationary in the air, before turning a full three hundred and sixty degrees, and travelling back along the route it had taken, once again becoming stationary at around the location opposite us. It then turned to the north again, and as it disappeared behind the first Simpson Desert sand dune, there was a pink glow, and I realised we had a disaster on our hands. I must make mention here that several of our party, including Peter Young, said later that they had observed what appeared like an orange glow under the helicopter, that had become bigger and bigger as it disappeared behind the dunes. If just highlights the discrepancies that can occur in any eyewitness event, making the accident investigations that follow such events, so much more difficult.

What happened next is as follows. Peter and Rick together with two of our party (one, a nurse) headed off in one boat with a first aid kit. I straightaway rang the Port Augusta RFDS direct number, getting on to them immediately. I told them that the ABC helicopter had definitely gone down, and that we were going in to try and render assistance. I asked them to alert the police. They said they would, and asked me to contact them when we arrived at the site. Then, taking only my satellite phone, myself and the other *boatie* (Barry Peterson) headed off in my boat. There was still a slight glow in the northern sky, but it was fading fast, and I took a star sighting. Unbeknown to us, Peter and Rick had been held up by shallow water, but we had a better run and got across to the north shore in about ten minutes. We left the boat and started running toward the first sand hill, using my star for directions as the glow had faded altogether.

We reached the top of the first twenty metre dune, but there was only blackness in front of us. We kept running, but the country was rough and full of rabbit warrens and long haired rat holes, causing us both to fall several times. We realised that it was no sense one of us breaking something or spraining an ankle, so we slowed down to a fast walk. We crossed five or six dunes taking nearly half an hour, before observing a fire burning down on a flat. One of our real concerns was arriving at the crash site and finding one or more of the blokes shockingly burned, and us not being able to help them. As we approached the site, we began calling out in case anyone was alive, and maybe thrown clear, but there was no answer – just the fire burning with next to no other sound than the flames of the fire. We saw the frame of the helicopter, and soon realised that there was nothing we could do for the boys. While Gary searched the periphery of the crash site, I took photographs realising they would be valuable in the coming enquiry. Barry, who was ex Australian Air force, found the helicopter identification number. I straight away rang the Flying Doctor in Port Augusta, on the sat phone, and then the Port Augusta Police. They informed me that a police helicopter would be arriving at around two am.

Barry and I moved off the site to another little flat, where we lit a small fire as it was quite cold. Twenty minutes later the other party arrived. We told them the situation, suggesting there was no need for them to go to the site. I rang the police back, offering to stay at the site, but they said there was no need, and we began heading back to the camp. The nurse in our party was unaccustomed to this sort of hectic nocturnal travel and was pretty knocked up, so we took our time getting back to the water. It was after eleven when we finally arrived back at the camp. The whole party was obviously shocked, but people were handling the situation very well. I felt sort of numbed. One minute we were shaking hands and looking forward to the following day's events, and next thing we had lost three very good men.

We had a couple of rums and headed for our swags. What seemed like minutes later, the large rescue chopper overflew us, heading to the crash site, and around half an hour later was landing in our midst, creating a mini sand storm, and blowing loose gear everywhere.

A young, quite tall Star Force officer came over and took brief statements from Gary and I. There was also a very nice counsellor/nurse who offered counselling to anyone, but I told her that we were all okay, and half the crew were pretending to be asleep anyway. They also offered to fly anyone out, but no one wanted to go. The big chopper took off, heading for Marree. They had left two police officers at the crash site to secure the area. The Star Force bloke told me that other police would get full statements from us next day. We went back to bed again.

Next morning I rang the cops, and they told me we could depart, and that police would spend the next evening with us to get detailed statements. I gave them an approximate estimated location, and said that I would phone them our coordinates when we arrived at camp.

While all this was going on Patti was receiving non-stop calls from the media, and in the end she told them that I was un-contactable. Some of the calls were quite demanding, and she eventually stopped taking calls. I did an interview by phone that morning with ABC radio in Adelaide, and talked to one commercial journo flying with Trevor Wright. Then I refused all other phone requests for interviews.

Smoko time, we pulled in and climbed a high dune, having a minute's silence for the three blokes, which was the least we could do. My thoughts were for their immediate families who would be utterly devastated.

That afternoon I came to a suitable camp, and pulled in a kilometre or so in front of the other boats. Then a call on the UHF that Peter was having a *problem*, and could I come. I saw him pulled over to the opposite bank, and as I pulled up they were unloading gear out of the boat. It seemed that they had lost one of the bungs out of Peter's boat, and had taken in water. We sorted it out and went over to the camp, where I phoned in our coordinates to the Marree police.

A couple of hours later the rescue chopper arrived and without shutting down, dropped off two cops and a heap of gear, before lifting off and heading south. What occurred next was the only humorous event that we had experienced in the last day or two. I walked across to meet the two policemen, one being about 2 metres (six foot six).

As I walked up, something occurred that made me say "Gooday you blokes – I see you have brought your dog with you". Directly behind them, a dingo had materialised out of the low bush and was walking around behind them, several metres away. The big policeman, (James Klegg) had only been in Australia for a short time from the UK. His face was a picture with a look of absolute amazement. I'll never forget it. The dingo then sat on its haunches surveying the scene with interest. It had obviously had no contact with human beings, as is the case with most of the dingoes we see down here. It eventually sauntered off.

They spent the night with us, taking very detailed statements from all of the party. I must say that all contact with the SA Police concerning this situation, had been nothing but professional, and with a concern for the feelings of our party as well.

Next morning the chopper returned and the blokes flew out. The other constable was Mat Styles from Leigh Creek.

The CASA enquiry has been finalised, without coming up with a reason for the accident, which is unfortunate.

Dingoes are always good entertainment and a source of interest for us. On one occasion on the Warburton, two dingoes were swimming the river in front of us, and I got up alongside one of them. A lady leant over the side of the boat and scratched it on the back. I told her later it wasn't a real good idea, as she could easily have lost a hand. They have a massive bite for their size.

The modern day explorer (John Muir) had contacted me saying he was interested in having a go at crossing Lake Eyre. I had seriously considered having another go myself (we did in 1974) as the lake was over two thirds full in 2011. I was going to use my Zodiak using an electric pump that would suck water in and expel it from the back, creating motion that would get us through the mostly shallow water at the top end. Darren Wallace was coming with me. Then later, I favoured another idea, to borrow a local mate's special small *army duck* like machine that could not only travel through water, but mud as well. I needed to get a chopper in the region that was agreeable to pulling us out if we ran out of motion, but with all the bureaucracy that applies these days, none of the commercial companies would commit.

So I reluctantly gave the idea away, thinking that 1974 (the only time the lake had literally been full in European memory) was going to be a *one off*.

So John had rung, and I thought about it. Anyone else considering it I would have talked out of the idea. But here was a bloke who had done some amazing polar exploration, and climbed to the top of Mount Everest without the aid of sherpas. He had also walked across Australia with absolutely no assistance, living off the land as he went. A pretty amazing feat. A very unassuming bloke, who never made a lot of fuss. I agreed to help him where I could, and in due course met he and wife Suzie in their Canadian canoe on the river. Their amazing journey is written up in the Australian Geographic Magazine.

After a lot of trouble with wind and shallow water they managed to cross almost the full length of the Lake, finishing in Hallogen Bay, and getting out by vehicle via William Creek.

I have mentioned the Long Haired rats before, but I detail here a couple of standout incidents. Finishing one of our boat trips at Cowarie Station (Sharon Oldfield and family have given nothing but their full cooperation and help on our Warburton trips, as have Paul Broad and Jason Dunn on Etadunna concerning the Cooper trips).

We set up camp and later, sitting around the fire waiting for the evening meal, one of the ladies gave a startled shriek. She had a rather wide ornate wine glass, half full of wine sitting on the ground near her chair. The cause of her alarm was a rat, squatting on the rim of her glass, and guzzling the contents as fast as it could go! This rat obviously had a drinking problem, and we could have easily caught it. Billy had long since lost interest in rats.

Another time, before the Cooper had crossed the Birdsville track, we were camped on the shores of the dry Lake Killamperpunna on the way back from a Warburton trop. I was standing with the fire between myself and the Oka, that had the side up allowing access to the *kitchen department.* To my amazement, I saw a rat squatting in the back, looking at me. I went over and the rat disappeared into the gear in the back of the truck. We had a look next morning, and there was no sign of it. The next night we were camped at Warragundi, my property in the Flinders. I rolled my swag out that night, next to the side of the Oka. Up until around midnight I could hear something chewing in the back. Next morning, cleaning the vehicle out we found where something (the rat) had eaten a hole in the very hard plastic lids of one of the food tubs. It would have to have stood on its hind legs to get access to the lid. Imagine the difficulty in that. But despite a good look, no sign, and reckoned the Flinders Ranges might get another species on its fauna list.

I was home a day or two later in my office, when Patti called out to me from the shed. I went out, and she was holding up a weetbix packet. "Have a look what I have in here!" she said. One Long Haired rat! I noticed it was a male. So on the strength of it being the cheekiest and probably most travelled of its species, I let it out in the bush, where it disappeared from sight, and I haven't seen it since.

It had been a memorable three years, and who knows when the next navigable water will run down the sand beds of those famous rivers.

8
A COORONG CRUISE

With the Murray River running into the sea non-stop for over two years after the prolonged drought, 2012 saw the Coorong higher than it has been since the early nineties.

With fresh water prevailing around fifteen kilometres down the Coorong from the Murray Mouth, and with New Zealand Fur Seals in abundance in the North lagoon of the Coorong. This in itself was good enough reason to operate another boat trip along this unique South Australian *coastal treasure.*

I wrote of other boat journeys on the huge Lake Alexandrina and Coorong in 'Boats in the Desert', but this short account describes a six day boat safari undertaken in October 2012.

Three vehicles converged on the Milang bakery (worth a visit) on the southern shores of Lake Alexandrina, one of the iconic *Lower Lakes.* A description that has gained acceptance during one of the two worst droughts in the European settlement of Australia. During that difficult period hardly a day went by without the desperate plight of these Lakes being mentioned in the South Australian daily newspaper, The Advertiser.

The vehicles consisted of my Oka 4WD towing a large boat trailer carrying two of my heavy duty punts, with fuel and gear on board. On top of the Oka was a Zodiac inflatable (our *trailer*) and in the back of the Oka were stores and grog for a week. I had left home on the Murray near Weston Flat nearly four hours earlier.

A mate, Rick Moore, was in his new Mazda 4WD dual cab carrying four of our party, and minutes later Brenton Hicks pulled up in his Toyota HiLux carrying the last participant, as well as Ross Smith to drive the Oka and Mazda to Woods Well on the lower Coorong where I planned to finish.

Our party consisted of Kate Merry from Perth, Nick Wendt and Alan Tapper also from Perth, Alan's sister Marian Tapper from Melbourne, and Ann Pye from Alice Springs.

After a 'smoko' at the bakery, we drove the short distance to the small settlement of Clayton where we unloaded, and loaded (with gear) the boats. Brenton and crew headed off with the vehicles, and we motored half a kilometre and pulled into a nice little lunch camp on an unkempt *lawn* of native couch below a rugged fifteen metre cliff.

I was driving a 3.6 metre punt and Rick had a 4.2 metre, and was towing the Zodiac loaded with miscellaneous gear.

Boating along through the islands on the bottom end of Lake Alexandrina is an interesting experience. As you glimpse gaps between the islands and headlands, with no horizons, a sense of the size of this lake becomes apparent.

We travelled along massive reed beds, which would give protection if the wind were too strong. The day was warm and sunny, with a light souwesterly raising 15 centimetre waves that were no problem for us. Should they get above 60 centimetres, we would be looking for shelter.

Around four thirty we arrived at the Tauwitcherie barrage at the manually operated small lock on its north-west end. This is a quaint device where the public can operate a number of valves to get the craft into the lock chamber, and then out into the Coorong. Good fun had by all. We then crossed the half a kilometre or so to the Younghusband Peninsula, to our first camp.

The Coorong is tidal down to around Long Point (28km from the Mouth), and with a low tide we had to lug our swags etc. through low water and mud to a protected little campsite amongst Wisteria and Boobialla shrubbery. Wind is never far away in this part of the world and it was blowing quite hard as evening approached. There were plenty of mozzies, but we use insect domes this time of the year, which guarantees a mosquito free sleep.

Next morning with slightly more water we got under way and motored up to the Murray Mouth, passing a number of camps and other boats. A line of white water at the mouth marked the coming together of Murray River and Southern Ocean. A far more happier scene than the recent drought years when constant dredging was required to keep the mouth open.

We turned around and heading back down the Coorong saw a couple of New Zealand Fur Seals. This species, first seen here in March 2007, has been increasing each year since then. It has almost wiped out some colonies of Fairy Penguins (not in the Coorong). According to Gary Hera-Singh (Coorong fisherman) there is no historical presence of New Zealand Fur Seals in the Coorong middens, whereas kangaroos, etc, and interestingly, dingoes are well represented. They are causing ongoing problems for the fisherman, with culling not on the agenda.

At a lunch camp we found the remains of an Eastern Water Rat, the fur of this one a rich brown, rather than the greyer shades normally seen.

We made a good mile that afternoon, but had numerous encounters with the dreaded *bombies* – mounds of gritty sand and weed lurking just below the surface (formed by tube worms – these increased to plague proportions in Lake Alexandrina during the drought, causing encrustations on the backs of tortoises, killing hundreds), which pull you up very smartly on occasions. You get off them with a combination of pushing the boats, *poling* with paddles and long handled shovels, using the motors – and cursing!

That afternoon, the wind blew strong from souwest, and we headed for a 'camp' consisting of a solid hut and a caravan. Not easy getting in to shore, and when water shallow enough, the boats have to swing around smartly with bows to the sea to avoid water coming over the back – a problem you don't usually have in the desert, except when on Lake Eyre.

I went over to the camp where I met John, a shy man, but as it proved shortly, a very hospitable one. He asked us inside his large hut, consisting of one main room, and enquired if we would like a drink. Several of us answered in the affirmative, and sampled some excellent homemade port and brandy. Some continued *sampling* while the rest of us brought out the Bocce balls and played a closely contested game on the native couch *lawn*.

Gary Hera-Singh used this location as a fishing camp and one of his dinghies was moored out the front. It was a tricky crossing (sandbars and rocky reefs) to the Younghusband side where I wanted to camp, so John got Gary on the phone. He gave me some good advice, and we prepared to cross rough water. John put on his waders and helped us *get off* the shore. In around twenty minutes we were moored at *Lousy Jacks,* one of the best *camps* on the Coorong.

It came with a nice beach and a flat sandy area covered in native couch. There was a stand of Tuart Gums, some dead and some alive, which were planted years ago in a number of spots by fishermen. This stand would probably now be the highest trees on Younghusband Peninsula, up to around twenty metres.

Just after dark, Gary Hera-Singh arrived by boat, and we spent a very pleasant couple of hours. When he left, our party knew a lot more about the Coorong than before he arrived.

When professional fishing was finally prohibited on the Murray (2003), the future looked very bleak for the Coorong fishermen. However they presented a united front, and received accreditation for sustainable and well managed fisheries, from the International body, the Marine Stewardship Council. Consequently the public are still able to enjoy the delicious Coorong mullet, a species found nowhere else. It is rare to be able to catch any Coorong fish by line or rod, due to the turbidity of the Coorong water. Strictly nets, and only professional fisherman are able to use nets these days.

Next morning was overcast with flat water and we made good time, averaging about seven kilometres per hour.

A *smoko* on the *mainland* side of the Coorong, where Marian saw a small snake, the only one encountered on the whole trip. Surprising, as Younghusband Peninsula had a lot of Eastern Brown Snakes in particular. Tiger snakes are rarely found in the Coorong area, once you get beyond the barrages, whereas they are very common around the lakes, feeding mainly on frogs and small invertebrates.

Brenton Hicks, at Jockwar Station on Lake Alexandrina, would arguably have more snakes in the vicinity of his homestead than anywhere else I have experienced in Australia – both Tigers and Eastern Browns.

Next camp was at a location where the Younghusband Peninsula was only about a kilometre wide.

Next morning, taking a couple of surf casting rods, a bucket and our *smoko,* we made our way through the thick low scrub to the Ninety Mile Beach. A wild and remote place, considering its relatively close proximity to Adelaide. A three metre wall of almost vertical sand was between us and the beach, and much fun was had as each of us slid to the beach on our bums. All kids at heart, which is the only way to be.

We spent the morning there, bird watching, fishing and cockling. The latter produced good results, with cockles (or *pippies*) 5 centimetres under the sand on the waterline, and we soon had a bucket full as was required. A few pied oystercatchers, silver gulls and several waders was all the ornithology we were going to get, and the fishing didn't produce a bite, but it was a good place to be.

We headed back, visiting an open area of around half an acre, littered with the fractured shells of thousands of cockles. Unlike the usual high piles of the middens, but because of its sheltered location, no doubt an important aboriginal location in years gone by.

The warm afternoon was spent in the meagre shade of the low vegetation reading, yarning, sleeping and swimming. That evening the cockles provided our hors d'oeuvres.

Earlier, Alan had seen a White Bellied Sea Eagle, which was a good addition to our bird list. Because of the increased salinity due to reduced flows in the Murray, the massive flocks of *waders* are a thing of the past. Experienced estimates are as low as 20% of numbers regularly seen each year in the latter part of last century. An ecological tragedy. However numbers of many species have increased since the drought.

We set off on calm water and soon arrived at *the Needles,* a narrow shallow part of the Coorong with several islands. This divides the north lagoon from the south lagoon, and prevents most boats from travelling on. I remembered a lot of strife here before, pushing boats, and wishing I was somewhere else. Gary Hera-Singh had given me a good *mud map* of our route, and with the additional help of Larry Hayward (a retired Coorong fisherman whose very interesting homestead is only metres from the Coorong shore).

We had lunch on one of the islands, and while there, were greatly entertained by a lone emu. It appeared about two hundred metres away to the south, walking toward the water. It waded matter-of-factly into the Coorong, and when the water was well above its knees, it suddenly lay down, and proceeded to kick out its legs. It rolled around for eight or ten seconds kicking its legs out again, before standing up and shaking itself vigorously. Its tail feathers had a pronounced *droop*. It then walked to shore and disappeared into the bush. Great *floor show*!

Once through the Needles, the water was mostly deeper and we made good time. Later in the afternoon we came to the Coorong Wilderness Resort, located at *Hells Gate* the Coorong's narrowest point. The restaurant is shaped like a flounder (flat bodied fish). We pulled in here, went up and had a coffee, which is something you can't do when you're half way down Cooper Creek! It is owned and operated by the local Ngarrindjeri people, and like Camp Coorong, is a well-run and interesting operation. We had hoped to incorporate a bush tucker walk back at Camp Coorong but the weather conditions didn't allow it.

We passed a string of islands, and with high winds and a very wide part of the Coorong coming up, we pulled into a protected spot on Long Island. A protected camp was soon established, and we rolled our swags out rigged for rain.

Next morning I poked my head out of my swag watching the 60 centimetre waves rolling into the beach and decided we wouldn't be moving. Rain was threatening so in the next hour or so we rigged up a large *hootchie* over a couple of very large currant bushes, and we enjoyed a nice snug camp on a windy day with intermittent showers of rain. Walking, eating, reading and talking were the order of the day.

The Coorong is a national treasure, but it is degraded in many aspects. Noxious weeds are a big problem, the two real standouts being box thorn and false caper. The islands are badly affected, and both shorelines, particularly the eastern side. It wouldn't take massive funding for the relevant authorities to get the islands and the Younghusband shoreline in particular back to near original condition. Some replanting of many of the salt tolerant species such as ruppia, vital as water bird habitat are being planted as part of a large Government revegetation program.

Later that afternoon Rick saw four western grey kangaroos hopping, equally distanced between our Island and theisland to the north, through about 60 centimetres of water.

The next morning, and our last day, there was very little improvement in weather. But we had to go. There was around eight kilometres to travel and it was going to be far from pleasant. I must say, from an operator's point of view, it makes a huge difference to have a *tight* little party.

Fair enough, no one was going to drown, but there was always the possibility of a boat being swamped (tinnies can't sink because of the inbuilt flotation). We get pretty handy at operating heavily loaded tinnies to the max, but you don't look for trouble.

So we got off the beach with difficulty, relieving the Coorong of some of its water, and made our way steadily into the 76 centimetre waves. We were doing okay, but my 3.6 metre boat (all our other boats are 4.2 metres, and much more stable in these conditions) began taking water over the stem. I had Mick Wendt, an ex-station man who relished a challenge, at the back, and moving the fuel tank forward he began bailing with a 4 litre bucket. This kept us honest, particularly as we had to turn towards Woods Well, and taking the waves a third of the way down our starboard sides. We took the boats behind a small island, and ran out of water, but this gave us a chance to bail out properly.

We headed off again, and with the three houses and trees of Woods Well getting ever closer, rode the waves in until we grounded – a good feeling.

There are easier ways to experience the Coorong (top end) like on one of Jock Veenstra's well-run cruise boats operating out of Goolwa. But by the party's body language, this little *warts and all* boat safari ticked most of the boxes.

P.S. A cynic might argue that the party's *body language* was just an indication of their relief at arriving at Woods Well! You be the judge.

9

GREAT VICTORIA DESERT CAMEL EXPEDITION

(PLUS GETTING THERE AND COMING HOME)

I had organised a 32 day Great Victoria Desert camel expedition to begin in early July 2010. Originally I was going to lead it myself but with the Warburton and Cooper rivers running into Lake Eyre needed to keep focused on my boat safaris.

So I pulled Johnny Whittaker out of *mothballs* to lead it. He had worked for me for nearly thirty years on and off as a cameleer, and had also owned his own camel trekking business. In my opinion one of the best Australian cameleers alive today. He grew up around Coorabie on the Great Australian Bight, much of his childhood spent with the aboriginal kids at Yalata. A fishing skipper, opal miner and other varied bush occupations all go together to making him the very good bushman he is today.

Ryan MacMillan who began working for me with camels some five years earlier was his offsider and Ryan's girlfriend, (now wife) Natalie (a biologist) was the other staff member.

Several of the camels on this trip belonged to Ryan and I had given him some others as he was going to contract them and himself to me the following year.

There was a party of twelve people some of them having travelled with me previously. Actually getting camels, people and gear to the starting point of an expedition is often something of an expedition in itself.

So Rick Moore, in his Nissan Patrol wagon, myself and Patti (and Jack Russell terrier *Billycan*) in our Oka 4WD left Morgan with the camel party. We arrived in Copley where we had to meet Roger Redpath who was loading camels that morning at Angepena Station, in the middle of the Flinders Ranges, between Copley and Balcanoona. This is the widest part of the Flinders, a distance of a hundred kilometres.

A few days earlier Ryan and Natalie had walked some of the camels from Arkaroola (where Ryan and Natalie work) to Angepena. John Whittaker had been dropped off at Angepena the night before loading by AJ, his partner. Sounds complicated, and it was.

My party began having lunch at the Quandong Café in Copley, and were just finishing that when the semi arrived. We watched as it drove around the other side of the railway to and old earth loading ramp. That was a bit unusual. After about ten minutes when no one had come over to the café, I noticed there seemed to be a problem at the truck and walked over. There was a problem all right. *Jacko,* a big white coloured bullock had put a foot through the floor of the tray (not Roger's fault but too long a story to go into here). There was no damage to the camel, so we presumed it had just happened – unless he had been holding it up off the road while travelling.

We then had to unload the whole fifteen camels (a demoralising job, because loading camels is both physically and mentally draining). There were several freshly broken camels, and great care had to be taken because of the danger of them *bolting.*

When the camels were off, one of the boys had scrounged a piece of thick ply from a Copley backyard and the floor was temporarily repaired.

It's worth mentioning here that if the animal in the predicament had been a horse, it quite likely would have had to have been shot and then dragged bodily out with a vehicle. A good example of the difference in temperament between a horse and a camel.

Finally, by mid afternoon the camels were reloaded, and the three vehicles headed north for Marree with the semi leading.

We camped after dark near Lake Eyre South, after collecting a few old railway sleepers for a fire. The usual first night feed of chicken, salads, and apple pie were consumed, before all in sundry headed for their swags. It had been a long day.

Up at daylight next morning and on the road an hour and a half later, to William creek, across to Coober Pedy then up the Stuart Highway to Marla, where we turned off for the Mintabie opal fields. The camels had travelled well, but as always it was a relief to reach the old airstrip near Mintabie and get them unloaded.

We tied them to various feed trees and bushes while the gear was unloaded and sorted, a long and complex job, but one we were well used to. Then another meal, bed, and up before daylight next morning.

As with most extended camel expeditions, it took a full morning before the camels were loaded and ready to go. They finally walked away into the mulga scrub about one thirty, and Rick, Patti and I were ready to drive home in the two four wheel drives. As we drove off I told Rick on the UHF radio not to look in his rear vision mirror (we left at the same time that the camels walked away)

As it turned out the camels lost a load in the first five minutes! But we didn't know about it. It was a bit of a novelty for me to be in the vehicles and not with the camels.

32 DAY CAMEL EXPEDITION

Not being on the camel expedition, I am relating here two incidents that occurred, as described to me by John Whittaker (leader) and Owen Davies, a mate of mine who was one of the party.

Camel expeditions vary a lot. Like most of our *long haul* expeditions since 1976, this one traversed some areas where no European had set foot.

We have always had to shoot feral bull camels for our own safety but this journey was exceptional in that over twenty had to be destroyed. More than any trip in the past due to the explosion in feral camels.

In recent years, I have written about this in my other books, particularly *Outback by Camel.*

In the last week of the expedition, one of our older male camels started to *break down,* and eventually had to be abandoned. Though rarely occurring, it's a very sad situation for all concerned. Its packsaddle and load were carried on.

A few nights later at about eleven pm, the party were awakened by wild camels in the camp, around a dozen or so. Young bulls. One was shot, and the others dispersed.

John was settling his camels down when he realised the string had an extra member! A large young bull was standing with some of our camels, and when approached showed no sign of fear, and just walked away some metres. John watched him while Ryan went away and came back with a long rope. They moved some string camels around the bull, and then what John did next took a lot of guts and a degree of luck.

With a long forked stick and the rope, he moved quietly through the camels until he was near the bull, who was standing still and shaking slightly placing the end of the rope over the forked stick, he gingerly fed the rope over the bulls neck until it reached the ground. The, abandoning the stick he crawled under one of the string camels until he could reach the rope. Tying a bowline knot around the bull's neck, he tied the other end to a tree, before moving the quiet camels away. The bull went mad, throwing itself around, and pulling hard on the rope. They watched him for a while, before heading for their swags.

Next morning the bull was still tied, and the nearby string camels were very nervous. Taking two of our stronger camels, (Bonny and Jacko) John tied the bull to Bonny and walked the three into camp, and tied the bull to another tree. They loaded up and headed off with two strings of camels. Ryan led the short string with the bull on the end, with John giving him some *tuition* along the way. At one stage the bull (now called Victor) walked the wrong side of a large Black Oak tree, resulting in a huge tangle up that took a while to sort out.

Then Victor's rope broke and the circle of camels were put around Victor while John repeated the process of getting a rope on him.

That night Victor was tied down and John put hobbles on him (front legs) before *teaching him a few more tricks.* A packsaddle was put on him next morning, with pack bags loaded with sand. Victor had trouble jumping up with his hobbles on, but when removed he soon got the hang of it.

While packing up was taking place, Victor was left standing (in his hobbles) with the other camels. He seemed quite settled. Soon after, it was noticed that he was missing. He was tracked and could be seen where he was cantering in his hobbles at some stages. After seven or eight kilometres he was finally back in the mob.

After that he just settled into full time employment with the Bush Safari Co, improving every day. By the time the second trek finished at the Railway, Victor was a valuable asset in the transport department.

THE SEARCH

The day before I was due to arrive on the scene to swap parties, another *drama* occurred – one that if not for the good bushmanship displayed, could very easily have ended in tragedy, or precipitated a public search - neither a good result for the party.

The expedition was heading for a *road* where the camel/vehicle rendezvous was to take place.

Rob was an old friend of mine who had been on many of my trips over the years, including camel treks in the Flinders Ranges. A dairy farmer, he was solid and reliable. However, this was a day that he will definitely want to forget.

The *string* was underway, and at around ten in the morning Owen Davies had reason to come from the front of the string, where he normally walked, around to the rear. He saw and talked to Rob, who said he had walked off to take a photograph and became disorientated in the featureless Mallee/Spinifex country. Owen put him on what we call the *spiderweb* (the tracks of the camel string) and carried on with whatever he was doing. Owen said that he would let him walk along at his own pace, while he would jog up to the front of the string to resume his place as *pointer* (walking with the compass). He let John (Whittaker) know of Rob's position at the rear.

When the camels pulled up for lunch just before midday, it was noticed that Rob wasn't present. As lunch was had, the party became increasingly concerned, and John lit a small *smoke fire*. However, there was a wind blowing and the smoke stayed low and dissipated.

At around one thirty Owen, Ryan and Natalie began a search. Ryan and Natalie walked back along the tracks, while Owen scouted out to the side, but in touch. Ryan carried a camel bell so they could keep in touch, and hopefully for Rob to hear.

They met back where the party had crossed the road, a distance of around five kilometres. They could see where Rob had been disorientated after taking his photographs, and then tracked him along the fresh camel tracks (the *spiderweb*). They hadn't gone far when the new tracks crossed other camel pads, at least two weeks old. They could see where Rob had mistakenly followed this. What should have been a relatively straightforward tracking operation was soon complicated by a lot of hard ground. In addition they found several places where Rob had circled around looking for the expeditions tracks, realizing by now that he was in strife. Eventually, around midday, Rob did the wise thing and stayed put.

Meantime the situation was becoming more confused for the trackers. They backtracked to where Rob had left an arrow marked on the ground, but this gave them no useful clue. Owen took off his boots as their tracks were adding to the confusion because of the backtracking.

At around five pm, and with constant ringing of the bell, Rob's tracks were picked up heading west.

Regrouping, Owen began jogging, all the time focussing on Rob's tracks, and soon after heard a *cooee*. Ryan responded with a similar call, and within minutes Rob could be seen walking towards them. A very relieved group. Throughout, Rob had remained calm and said that he had prepared a *camp* for an overnight stay.

The GPS showed they were 2.7 kilometres from the camel camp and they set off arriving just after dark.

One of those situations that all concerned will not forget in a hurry.

THE RETURN SERVICE RUN

Three days before the camel expedition was due to finish, I left in the Oka with three passengers, overnighting at a motel in Port Augusta. These three people would make up the party of a twenty day expedition, to be led by Ryan MacMillan. It would finish on the Trans Australian Railway line, where Roger would pick camels and gear up in his semi, and transport them back to the Flinders Ranges.

At Ceduna, I was joined by Murray Collins and Bill Tonkin, both having operated other 'service runs' with or without me before. They were farmers, and very used to driving around the bush.

As we headed west along the Eyre Highway we were running into weather. That night we were due at Cook, up on the railway line and we were keen to get there ahead of the rain. Just before we turned off the Eyre Highway for Cook, I got Murray to throw some old fence posts in the back of his Toyota, as I'm allergic to travelling anywhere without wood.

It started raining lightly when we were half an hour from Cook, and we arrived just before dark. Cook has been a virtual ghost town for some time. Stationary fettlers have long been replaced with mobile contractors responsible for the railways maintenance.

By arrangement we were able to camp in one of the old fettlers' houses, which though run down, still had most of its facilities, including tables and chairs. Gas to cook with and a hot shower, so we all felt very snug as the rain increased on the iron roof.

Next morning, after around 15 millimetres, we set off north across the Nullarbor on one of the many *wheel track roads*. Travel was *sloppy* on the flats, but we made as good a time as possible, with speed improving the further north you get, as you have a lot less limestone on the surface. The weather was on my mind. There was more forecast and I wanted to change the parties over and get back on bitumen as soon as possible. Several inches of rain could see us stranded for a week or more.

We had lunch near a limestone rock hole on the northern edge of the Nullarbor, before moving into the sand of the Great Victoria Desert.

Always a wonderful environment to travel through with a great variety of flora and fauna. I was keeping my eyes open for Scarlet Chested Parrots in particular, but didn't see any on this occasion. Passed half a dozen wild camels before reaching the camel camp about two pm. The first indication of that was Owen standing on the side of the track. We followed him about half a kilometre where we came across the usual conglomeration of gear with a group of very dirty (we prefer to say *dry cleaned* - by the elements) people. They looked a lot fitter, happier and healthier than when I had last seen them.

I inspected the new ruminating member of the string (Victor) and he seemed pretty happy in the service.

Within an hour we had unloaded new stores, people and water, and reloaded with the old party and gear. We headed south, making good time, and reached the edge of the Nullarbor Plain just before dark.

There were dark clouds to the west and I was keen to get back to cook before it rained again. We lit a fire on one of the dongas (depressions in the plain where there is more top soil, resulting in larger vegetation growth – like islands in a sea of salt and blue bush) and had a barbeque, before continuing on.

There had been rain over our tracks, and many of the flats were covered in water. The *flats* and low rises follow one another. The low rises, which are rougher going because of the limestone, were drier. After a few hours of mostly slow travel, the lights of Cook could be seen, and I felt confident of getting there before midnight. The rain had stopped, but I didn't know for how long.

And then it happened. I had just driven out of a long water covered flat, before emerging on to a small clay pan – it was wet but had no water on it. I was in second gear, four wheel drive high ratio and doing less than fifteen kilometres an hour. As my wheels contacted the wet clay, the Oka got into a moderate *slide,* something to be expected and often experienced in this type of driving.

I kept very minimal power on and *corrected* into the slide – as you do. Then I felt my near side rear wheel contact something, before everything seemed to go into slow motion. I realised the Oka was going to roll over, and couldn't believe it!

But it did, on to its side, at a very slow speed. I had taken my seat belt off twenty minutes before, and not put it back on. I felt myself flying through the air, and landed on Johnny Whittaker. I asked if he was okay and he replied that he would be if I would get off his -------- head. I heard Billy, my Jack Russell, who has a little *camp* under the rear seat, growling. It turned out a jack had fallen on him. I yelled out if everyone was okay and it seemed like they were.

I had never had a vehicle accident in my life, and felt a sense of unreality with the situation. I hauled myself off *Whittie's* head, stood up and opened the driver's door which was facing in the direction of the Southern Cross. I pushed it open, with difficulty, and climbed out, as the other two vehicles pulled up. Everyone, including Billy was okay, and in ten minutes all were out surveying the situation.

It wouldn't have been my choice of a camp, but we didn't have much option.

The old fence posts soon produced a roaring fire with tea, coffee and a port improving the outlook marginally. I think the camel party probably wondered why they weren't still travelling with camels!

We tried pulling the Oka on to its wheels with the two Toyotas, but things were too wet. That night I lay in my swag, wondering what tomorrow would bring. We were twelve kilometres north of Cook.

I woke up the next morning, and saw that it wasn't a bad dream. The Oka was still lying on its side. Murray, John and I hopped into Murray's Toyota and drove into Cook, taking about half an hour. The rain had gone.

We set about collecting pieces of old railway sleepers, and anything we reckoned might help us get the Oka on its wheels.

As we were about to drive out of town, we saw that a large flatbed truck was also leaving town – in the other direction. The other thing that we couldn't help noticing was that the said truck had a derrick (crane) on it. We pulled them up and it turned out to be a couple of blokes with the Railway Contractors. I suggested that there were tourist attractions to be had north of Cook, and not only that, instead of paying to see them, they would put account on the ward to see them. The blokes were keen, and after a satellite phone call to their boss, they were following us north across the sodden plain. It took us an hour to get back out there, but within ten minutes the Oka was on its wheels. We reloaded the roof rack, did the necessary mechanical checks, and fired it up.

Okas are R.O.P.S. (Roll Over Protection Systems) rated and the only damage was a slightly bent roof rack, and exterior passenger loading grip flattened, and the rear side rear vision mirror broken. I guess the vehicle hadn't *rolled over*, but *fallen over*. In the light of day, it was obvious what had happened.

Following the Okas tracks back about ten metres you could see where the near side rear wheel had gone over a deep wheel track that had been made in a previous wet time. The depth was about fifteen centimetres with the two sides pushed up setting almost as hard as concrete. It had been enough when connected by the sliding vehicle to put us over.

THE EXPENSIVE FILL-UP

If you think that was all the drama this service run had, well, you'd be wrong.

We drove into Cook, then had a very slow, wet drive down to the Eyre Highway. I called in and showed the party the whales at Head of the Bight, a nice contrast to the camels in the desert.

Then, back on the Eyre Highway heading for a mate's place (Spitter and Trina) near Port Sinclair on the Great Australian Bight – where we would stay the night.

It was just after dusk when I pulled into Nundroo Roadhouse to fuel up. A sign out the front said "Cheap Fuel" – I mention this because it is sort of relevant.

I will also mention that unbeknown to me, Colin Campbell and his young son, from Mundrabilla Station, were sitting in the roadhouse restaurant, having a steak and eggs. He was on one of his rare trips to Ceduna. Colin and I go back a long way.

I pulled up at the diesel bowser, and by now it was dark. Truck bowsers are equipped with longer than usual fuel hoses. I filled my near side tank, then pushed the filler hose under the Oka and filled the other tank. Then I went back around, pulled the hose back, and hung it back on the bowser.

At this junction I will mention the fact that the Oka has an air operated side step on the near side that drops down when you switch the motor off, and folds back up when you start the motor.

By now, the average reader should be visualising the scene.

I then went in and paid the bill, and came back out, hopped in the Oka, started up and drove off.

Right at this precise moment Colin Campbell paused with disbelieving eyes and fork full of steak half way to his mouth. We'll get back to him in a minute.

I drove off into the night, and had only gone about a kilometre, when I became aware of a vehicle behind me, flashing its lights and sounding its horn. I pulled over, walked around the front of the vehicle where I encountered a very excited Indigenous man. He said "You've got the bowser mate!" I looked and saw a foreign object protruding from the vicinity of the fuel tank, clamped by the automatic step, and disappearing into the darkness.

On further inspection I was hugely relieved that the bowser was not on the end of it! I thanked my pursuer and drove back to Nundroo where I was confronted by a European Australian (the Manager) who was actually a lot more excited than the Indigenous bloke. We eventually came to an arrangement, but of much more interest is Colin Campbell's account. Like I said, he was having a feed with his little mate, not anticipating anything out of the ordinary. Nundroo is Nundroo. However, things suddenly changed in that area.

He saw this white Oka multicab pull up, but didn't recognise it as mine, because I hadn't had this one long, and it had no sign writing on it.

When I walked into the roadhouse Colin must have been studying his plate, but when I hurried out to drive away, he recognised me. Before he could go outside, I was in the Oka and off. But what happened, kept him glued to his chair anyway. As I started up, what looked like a large mechanical hand seemed to reach out from under the vehicle, grabbing a fold of hose as it moved into its place.

I drove off, the hose was yanked from the top of the bowser, and as I disappeared into the night, diesel shot out the top of the bowser like a geyser! Dramatic entertainment that money couldn't buy.

Owen rushed into the servo and told them to switch the power off.

So much for cheap fuel. To cut a long story short it cost me over a thousand dollars!

10
ALONG THE ROCKY ROAD OF LIFE

WEDGETAILS

Wedgetailed eagles are the ultimate opportunists when it comes to getting a feed, anything from carrion to kangaroos. I have written about them in the past, but here are a couple of incidents that occurred recently.

A mate of mine, Garry Duncan, is an artist par excellence, and a very keen birder. He owns a large tract of mallee in the Riverland. A few months ago he was out there with some friends, and he cooked a sheep on a spit. The next day he returned, and found that a lot of the carcase had been pulled off the spit by eagles. There was a resident pair nearby and they were used to Garry. He cleaned the meat up, left one piece in a nearby mallee tree, and took the rest home so as not to encourage foxes. Over the next few months, every time he would go out to his block he would leave a piece of meat in the mallee tree. Just recently when he visited the block, there was a young eagle sitting in the mallee tree where the meet had been left. Garry walked up slowly, with a sheep *flop* in his hand, and the eagle didn't move. He walked right up, held the flap out and the eagle took it. How good is that?

Just a few days ago I was up at my block in the Flinders with my eldest grandson, Rainer, who is ten years old. It was very hot weather. The day we left, we visited an old mate (Tex) who lives in a stone hut at a beautiful location in the vicinity of the Parachilna Gorge. As we drove up to the hut a Wedgetailed eagle flew low in front of the vehicle, giving us a good view.

As I drove, Rainer said "the eagle has landed on the roof". I said that wouldn't be right, but when I looked there it was – sitting on the hut roof. I pulled up in front of the hut, and said to Tex, "Have you got a pet eagle?" We walked around the corner of the hut and there it was, sitting up about 9 metres away. It was a young bird, and showed no fear, staying there for ten minutes or so, before flying off and landing on the ground fifty metres away. Five minutes later it was a speck in the sky. Those are that sort of things that make your day.

OUTBACK SERVICE STATIONS

Like outback pubs, outback service stations often do a lot more for the travelling public (and locals) than dispense fuel.

One of the best examples I know is Hawker Motors in South Australia's Flinders Ranges. It was originally operated by Fred Teague, one of the *old school* bushmen. Prior to that he had many bush jobs, including driving the Birdsville Mail. His welcome would never vary. As well as giving excellent service he had a wealth of information on the Flinders Ranges.

Fred died a few years back, and his son John took over the running of it, with wife Janet. John is a chip off the old block, and the same helpful friendly service applies. When the periodic grasshopper plagues strike, he would be out cleaning people's windscreens with his special remedy. A rare sight these days.

Last year I injured my back, and my mate had to stand by my open door while I clamoured on to his back, before sliding slowly to the ground. John was watching with an amused look on his face, before joking that *he could give me a rub down*. That gave me an idea, so we set something up for the next trip in a week's time.

Before arriving in Hawker I had been singing the praises of Hawker Motors. When we pulled up (my back was still a bit stiff) I did the sliding off my mate's back bit, and as I hit the ground, Johnny Teague walks up, saying "Come over here Rex and I'll give you a rub down". I walked over to a garbage bin, half dropping my strides. John pulled my shirt up, took out some liniment, and began a back massage being quite serious about the process. My party were pretty impressed, and I just told them that any good service station would do the same!

During a recent heat wave, a New Zealand tourist pulled up in a Toyota Yaris. He had just changed a flat tyre, and his wheel was on its way off as he hadn't tightened the wheel nuts when the vehicle was lowered off the jack. John noticed the bloke was acting strangely, and recognised that he probably had a *touch of the sun*. He didn't have the particular tyre required, but could get it by the next morning. He suggested to the bloke that he book into a motel with air conditioning on and take it easy. The bloke was doing it cheap, sleeping in his car, and said he couldn't afford the motel. Then he said he needed fuel, took his petrol car to the diesel pump and filled it up. John had to drain it out. After that the bloke took off for Port Augusta without a spare wheel. Wasn't a lot more that John could do for him but it wasn't through lack of trying.

HUMPING IN THE NUDE

I had a phone call a couple of years ago from Rex Bate, who operates the pelican Point Nudist Caravan Park at Lake Bonney (Barmera).

He inquired into the possibility of bringing a party of nudists on a one day camel trek, and I said that would be no trouble at all. He suggested that I could leave my clothes home as well, but I declined the offer. Didn't really have a good excuse then, but I would now – you can bet your life occupational health and safety would have a law against it. The mind boggles.

I said to my offsider that the only way we were going to get through the day, was to avoid eye contact with each other. Nudists are very serious about what they do, and we didn't want to upset anyone. I also made sure that I removed every single burr out of the sheepskin saddle covers!

The party of nine duly arrived, fully clothed. When we headed off, they were still fully clothed. It was a hot day. The trip was quite *normal* until we reached our lunch camp on the river, but as soon as we stopped the party quickly became *deciduous*.

My mate Ian and I busied ourselves with preparing lunch, badly distracted by various *objects* periodically dangling above the platter as people helped themselves to food. There was no eye contact.

After lunch, everyone put their clothes on except for the youngest member of the group, a bloke in his mid thirties. He wore a bush hat and a pair of boots, and I have to say that very nearly brought me undone. I would have appreciated a bit of feedback from the camels.

When we got to the drying up Weston Flat lagoon, a remarkable spectacle unfolded. There were a lot of carp evident in the water that was less than 60 centimetres deep. All in sundry got off their humps and shed their garments like they were full of ants.

They each picked up a stout stick and line abreast (excuse the pun) they walked the length of the lagoon trying to dong the carp on the head. I am a keen photographer, but my professionalism kept me from using it, something I regret to this day.

We arrived back (clothed) and I think everyone enjoyed the day.

A month or two later I saw Rex, and asked him if they would do a repeat trip. Probably not, he said because the people were generally used to more *manicured* surroundings, like lawn and plenty of sand. Too many hazards out there for the uncovered. That was fair enough, but it was a memorable day for us.

PADDOCKS WITHOUT SHADE

Why is it that you never hear the RSPCA or anyone else for that matter, drawing attention to shadeless paddocks? Most farmers care about their stock, but how often do you drive through areas like the mid north of South Australia, and see sheep huddled together with their heads down desperately seeking shade. If there is a tree in the paddock, every centimetre of shade will be occupied.

Even if farmers don't care about the animals' comfort, they ought to realise that a happy animal is a healthier animal, which means more dollars in the long run.

All it takes is half an acre or whatever, to be fenced off in a paddock corner and a few trees to be planted. Ideally, native shrubs would be included so as to improve the biodiversity of the area – more native birds mean more dollars remember.

Increasingly hot summers could be on the agenda, so you live in hope.

PEACE ON THE RIVER

If you spend a bit of time on the Murray (in particular) and you are not a dedicated speedboater or jet skier, then these few paragraphs could be of interest.

I live right on the Murray, and even though it is a remote part of the river we get a few speedboats and jet skis going past – mainly on the holiday weekends in the summer. Speedboats I can live with, but there is something about jet skis that offends me to the core. I am aware of their value in such things as sea rescue, etc but as soon as they appear they blot out every other activity on the river. The riders seem to have the attitude that they are there to entertain, and will invariably flaunt themselves in front of other river users in their noisy and mindless displays.

So one morning I was having a cuppa with an old mate of mine in one of the Riverland towns. He was one of the original batch of Special Air Service (SAS) personnel formed soon after the Korean war. I had known him for a long time, working with him in the bush years ago. You could argue that he was a bit of a *wild man*, but a very competent one.

I was complaining to him about how speedboats and particularly jet skis were annoying me on occasions, and he replied "Mate, you don't have to put up with that". I said "Jack, you can't shoot them!" He just smiled and said "No, you don't have to do that".

He told me that you get a roll of industrial strength glad wrap and at an opportune time, and string it across the river. It sits just under the surface, and looks about the colour of Murray water. When anything with a jet motor passes over it, many metres of glad wrap is sucked up, and once more you can hear the cackle of a darter, or the flute-like notes of a pied butcher bird.

It doesn't damage motors – just puts them out of action for several hours and the owners of these machines, spend a lot of time cursing *pollution* in the River Murray.

So I thought I would give it a go. Early one morning I was out in the tinny, and strung the said material across the river. It was a long weekend, and there were a few *irritants* in the vicinity.

However, an hour after I had completed the job, a wind got up and the glad wrap let go on the other side of the river. It blew it over my side of the river, where it broke in a few places. That evening I collected it up (as I always would). I haven't tried it since, but there will come a day.

DINGOES

Over the years I have had a dual relationship with this ultimate Aussie survivor. On various sheep stations in the 1960s it was part of my job to destroy dogs, and I have shot and trapped a number of them.

In the last couple of years they have become a very real problem in the Flinders Ranges and adjacent pastoral country, due partly to sections of the dog fence being washed away with floods. Running my camel treks through the Flinders, I wouldn't hesitate to shoot them if the opportunity presented itself, as they threaten the very existence of station owners, and indeed the entire sheep industry. At least one station has changed to cattle, after over a hundred years of running sheep. All across Australia from north of Kalgoorlie in W.A. to the Great Dividing Range, dingoes and wild dogs are threatening graziers.

However, I also have a very positive relationship with dingoes, due to over forty years travelling with 4WD vehicles, camels and boats in Australia's remotest areas. When pure bred dingoes have had no negative contact (ie. being shot at or chased by vehicles) with humans, they will very often approach within metres of a person or party. I have many examples of these *close encounters*. One *classic* involved a mate of mine working for a mining company, and camped out on the Officer Creek in NW South Australia. He had his swag on a stretcher (a *softie*) with the foot end of the stretcher just a couple of metres from his campfire. It was late winter, but a Front was passing over causing humid conditions. Through the night he pushed a blanket off his swag, half on to the ground at the bottom of his stretcher. In the early hours, it became colder, so he half sat up and went to pull the blanket back over his swag. It wouldn't come, so he gave it a *yank*. There was a startled yelp, and a dingo jumped up and headed for the bush. It had been asleep on his blanket as well as being warmed by the coals of the campfire!

In 2000, or 2001, I was travelling in boats down the Warburton River to Lake Eyre. My current Jack Russell, at the time, (Stubbie) was sitting on the front of my boat. We rounded a bend and there were three dingo pups on a little mud island several metres from the bank. They jumped into the river and swam to the bank disappearing into the lignum. Stubbie straightaway jumped into the river heading for the spot where the pups disappeared. I quickly ran the boat into the bank, worrying about the parents of those pups who could easily make mince meat out of a Jack Russell.

I pushed my way through a few metres of thick lignum, before breaking out into a clearing the size of a couple of tennis courts. An amusing sight met my eyes. Stubbie was pursuing one of the dingo pups around the outside of the clearing, with the other two in line chasing him! No sign of the parents. The pups on seeing me disappeared into the lignum, and I grabbed Stubbie and headed back to my boat.

On a number of occasions, dingoes swim across the river in front of our boats, giving excellent photographic opportunities, and exciting close encounters if you can get up alongside before they get to the bank. A couple of months ago on the Warburton we came across two dogs swimming across, one about six metres behind the other. I sped up, and could have cut off the second dog, but it was older and having trouble keeping up with the lead dog, so I took pity on it and slackened off. A few days later a lady in front of one of the other boats, actually touched the back of a swimming dog. A bit *naughty* because she could have lost a hand. Dingoes have a massive *bite,* as well as very large feet for their size, and are excellent swimmers.

In 2009 on a desert river I saw a dingo running parallel with the river, carrying a weeks' old pup in its mouth. It plunged into a small creek running into the river, swam across holding its head high with the pup just out of the water, before scrambling out the other side and into lignum. A highlight for anyone's day.

On other occasions when crossing deserts in vehicles we have seen them trailing behind slow moving 4WDs climbing steep sand dunes, sniffing the exhausts, maybe getting hooked on carbon monoxide! Or walking up to a stationary vehicle and urinating on a wheel. Takes your mind off anything else at the time.

While we can't afford to relax our vigilance where the dingo is concerned, I hope these few accounts give an insight into a fascinating and successful predator for its own sake. No matter what your outlook, there will be no such thing, in years to come, as a pure bred dingo, as they will inevitably be interbred with *wild dogs*.

LOSING A DOG

Most of my life I have had a dog or dogs. When your family grows up and moves on, your dogs move up a notch and become your proxy family, to varying degrees. In Patti's and my case, it is very much so, as we live in a relatively isolated situation on the Murray river, in the semi desert of South Australia.

For the past twenty odd years we had two Jack Russells at any one time. *Bigger* was in her twentieth year, which is not unusual for Jack Russells. I know of one that was twenty five when it died. Mostly this breed dies of *misadventure* a lot earlier than that. My first one (*Trouble*) had died of snake bite in our back yard, at two years of age, and my next one (*Stubbie*) had been stolen when he was eight years old. My current dog was *Billycan* and he was six years old. Bigger had become Patti's dog, being her companion when I was away running trips. She would come on some trips when Patti was on them.

The last couple of years her sight and hearing had deteriorated, but she was still reasonably fit and healthy. However, we couldn't take here on commercial trips anymore, and having her looked after at home was becoming increasingly difficult. She was a much loved old dog, and you did what it took.

Most nights before we went to bed we would let her out the front door, where the house faced the river. The cliff edge was only thirty metres away. She would poke around out there, do her toilet, and come back and stand by the front glass door, and we would let her back into the house.

On this particular night, we both forgot about her, and when we looked, could see she wasn't standing by the door. Getting the torch we went outside to look for her. As I walked toward the cliff, I saw her about fifteen metres away, trotting along the very edge of the cliff. Being alarmed, I moved towards her, and as I did so, she suddenly moved to the left, and disappeared over the edge of the cliff. I ran forward and heard a *thud* and a second or two later a splash. I yelled to Patti and ran down our cliff track to the pontoon. I saw Bigger floating in the current, obviously dead. I could have retrieved her from the river, but as Patti arrived I said "Just let her go – let the river take her". We were both deeply shocked and upset. All her life, (Bigger) she had been a *goody two shoes*, and even in death she had done the right thing.

After a few days when we had recovered somewhat, we realised that by this tragic dramatic death she had eliminated the situation of a drawn out, difficult end to her life with the attendant problems that aging dogs have. We miss her a lot, but at the same time feel grateful to the dear old dog for the way she ended what had been a very good life.

Camp on Tumpawarrina Creek – Kallakoopah Creek

Kallakoopah Creek

Kallakoopah Creek. Early morning reflections.

'Big John" and Patti, Cooper Creek.

Reflections Warburton River.

Photographing wedgetailed eagles nest, Cooper Creek

Red cliff, Warburton River. Early morning light.

Long haired rat with a drinking problem.

Reloading camels at Copley.

Crow and Mishy, Great Victoria Desert camel Expedition.
Photo: Lyn Murray-Walker.

Warragundi, Flinders Ranges.

A fair dinkum outback service station.
Photo: Barry Peterson.

Young wedgetailed eagle on hut. Flinders Ranges.

Shallow water, Bulloo River.

Bulloo River.

Lachlan River.

Eastern Grey kangaroo having swim. Lachlan River.

Unloading boats, Strzelecki Creek

Canoe tree in background with old ladder used by Aboriginals to cut it out.
Murray River.

Barn Owl. Warburton River.

Camp in Strzelecki Desert.

'Dromedary' at Menindee Weir.

Dingo. Cooper Creek.

'Dromedary' on the Darling Moored near huge river Red Gum.

"Midnight Martini' playing at the 70th party.

Ps Renmark & barge at Netley Homestead (Bindara) 1934.
Photo: Bill & Barb Arnold.

'Dromedary' passing under Pooncarie Bridge.

Negotiating a submerged weir. Darling River Safari.

Our 'Stowaway' on the 'Dromedary'. A paddlewheeler up to the Darling.

11
BUREAUCRACY AND THE SHINY BUM DEPARTMENT

GUN LAWS

I want to tackle a subject that upsets and frustrates many country people in particular, but rarely gets an *airing* in public. People don't like to talk or write letters to the Editor about it for fear of being *targeted* – and that is wrong, and very un-Australian.

It is fair enough to have strict gun laws. Historically, like America, our pioneers, and settlers grew up with firearms always present and readily available. Unlike America, in Australia it was just accepted and understated, as is the Australian way.

It wasn't really until the Port Arthur massacre and John Howard's overreaction to the situation that the *problems* began. Politically, because most voters are in the cities, Howard's reaction was very popular, but not in rural areas, where the *good guns* were. Your average city dweller doesn't have a firearm these days, and are certainly not encouraged to.

A very different story in the country. People keep firearms for different reasons – to shoot feral animals, sporting shooting, hunting, trap shooting, duck shooting in some states still, target shooting, and for protecting ones family. The last item, you would think, would be your absolute right. But no, the *law* frowns upon it. Some *crazy* can violate your house, and if you dare to protect yourself, and even shoot the person dead, it is highly likely you will end up with a serious prison sentence. That fact is enormously resented, and it is unfair.

There's no argument about banning automatic weapons, particularly military weapons. But the law about *securing* your firearms causes great frustrations in the country. Leaving snakes and feral cats, etc out of it, I'll just concentrate on personal safety.

Of course it is common sense to keep firearms out of the reach of children, and any responsible parent does that. If someone wants to commit suicide with a firearm, they will get one. If they want to commit a robbery, or shoot an innocent person, they will easily get a firearm.

However, if a person wishes to protect their life or the life of a loved one, they have to go and get a key, then go to the gun cabinet etc, get the ammunition from another location, and only then are they able to resist the invader. Along with the majority of country people reckon that is downright stupid.

THE THINGS THAT ANNOY YOU

You could say that the things that annoy you, for most people, would come in two categories – major and minor.

In this instance, I want to concentrate on a few minor ones. Together they point to an increasing tendency for the *nanny state* to control our lives.

Australians, historically have resisted Government control, but with the ever increasing bureaucracy, more *controls* are forced on us. And like compliant sheep we allow ourselves to be *yarded up* – often so much without a *bleat*.

Here are a few examples.

DRIVING WITH YOUR LIGHTS ON

As we drive across this wide brown land, usually bathed in dazzling, often harsh sunlight, we periodically come across well entrenched signs, set in concrete. They instruct us, the passing motorists to *see and be seen*, in other words to put your lights on – even when the sunlight is so intense that to alight from your vehicle would see most wearing either a hat or sunnies. The inference, of course, is that to drive with your lights on during hours of sunlight is supposed to save lives. Therefore the *goody two shoes* put their lights on, in the smug belief that they are good responsible citizens. It's pretty pathetic.

If there was documented evidence that it was saving lives, well then you would have to consider going along with it. But there isn't, or I certainly haven't heard of any.

At the time of writing (end of 2012) it is not yet law – just the thin end of the wedge. Softening up the driving public, so that when the sufficient numbers are complying, they will pass it into law. And there will not be a whimper, even though thousands will be unhappy.

Now some might argue "what is wrong with driving with your lights on 24/7?" Well, I'll tell you what's wrong with it.

Speaking for myself (and I know thousands of others), I get a lot of pleasure from driving across the *Land of Oz*. I take in the ever changing countryside and its wildlife. Passing the occasional vehicle with its lights on is tolerable, though mildly annoying speaking for myself. But when you get a line of continuous traffic, I find it bloody annoying. The ambiance is shattered. If I am the only citizen to feel this I would be very surprised, and if I knew it to be the case I would shut up about it. In many cases the lights are on high beam, in your face and in itself comprising a hazard (albeit a mild one).

That's not to say that there are not occasions when you shouldn't have your lights on – like overcast dull conditions, heavy rain, etc. fair enough. Or, for dark coloured vehicles, they should definitely have lights on, on sunless days, or their parkers on all the time. Very often you are almost on a dark car on a dull day on bitumen before you see it. That is the exception.

A lot of modern cars come equipped with small driving lights. I could handle that as a compromise, but no, the powers that be will want the full Monty. So I am saying to the reader, if you don't want the rest of your driving life full of glaring headlights, speak up now before it's too late.

THE FLUORO SHIRT BRIGADE

These days, wherever you go you see working people clad in an array of gaudy bright clothing, usually red, orange, green or yellow.

Of course it's all to do with the all pervading Occupational Health and Safety. It dominates every workplace, and in many cases it's fair enough. Saves lives, so you can't argue with it.

But OH & S has long had the bit between the teeth, and in many cases makes the lives of many small business owners an ongoing misery with the attending paperwork. Many of the OH & S demands being totally irrelevant, but I'm not going to get bogged down in all that.

I just want to concentrate on the clothing. At the outset I would say that in many cases it is totally justified. For instance, for Murray River ferry operators in South Australia. In amongst traffic moving on and off the ferries, quite justified. Also for police directing traffic on busy intersections. All the obvious situations. But not for every truck driver and everyone else that is obliged by their companies to wear them. It's fine if the individuals are happy to comply, but only if they are happy. Here again, the reader may question my objection. Well it's all about self-esteem, and individualism.

A bloke might feel comfortable in say a khaki shirt, but his master decrees he must wear a glaring orange garment. It would annoy the shit out of me, I can tell you, particularly if, in so many cases, it was totally unjustified. The departments, that increasingly call the tune that we are supposed to dance to, love conformity. People that conform are easy to *yard up* or control, and that's what it's all about.

So what worries me is, why don't I ever see a letter to the editor, complaining about these imposts. Am I the only one that is questioning these things? I think not. Well if not, start writing letters. The silence is scary.

THE AUSTRALIAN LANGUAGE

The Australian Language is becoming a rare species, increasingly taken over by mostly *Americanisms*. Now, I am an admirer of the American language, but unless you are a Yank you shouldn't be using them. If you do you are compromising your Aussie identity. You are saying, "I would much prefer to be an American than an Australian". I have to admit, the Americans have a fine turn of phrase, but so have we, much of it based on Cockney, particularly the humour. A lot of particularly outback Aussies can talk in *strine* and eavesdroppers would not have any idea what the conversation is about. During the war it was the only *code* (used by the coast watchers) that the Japanese couldn't crack. How good is that?

I used to give my girls (daughters) a hard time for using the word *guys*. My eldest, Georgi, once said, "But Dad, you can call both males and females guys". My reply to that was to say, "Get an imagination – what's wrong with not being a sheep, and starting a new trend. You can call males and females *blokes*." But no, it's too hard. So I have more or less given up on *guys*, although I'll never use it myself.

It is really school teachers and radio announcers who bear the responsibility of safe guarding our language, and the great majority of them have let us down badly. Add to that group also, role models in all fields.

Unfortunately our population is mainly urban. Kids grow up in the suburbs without being exposed to the real Australian way of life, watching mostly American sourced television, etc, so we're up against it. The Yanks can teach us a lot when it comes to love of country, and living it. We have been in existence for a similar period, but their identity is arguably much stronger than ours.

Here's a few everyday words that have been hijacked and replaced with the Yank equivalent: *cookies* for *biscuits, guys* for *blokes, wrangle* for *muster* or *yarded up, buddy* for *mate* (that makes me cringe), *have a good day* for *see you later* or *hooroo,* and the list goes on.

ROADSIDE RAILING

Very necessary in many places, particularly steep banks, and no doubt has saved lives.

However, in the last few years steel roadside railinghas *bred up* in many places like an undulating, meandering tape worm stretching into the distance. The recently sealed Wilpena to Blinman road is a good example.

A huge cost to the tax payer, in many cases running along low banks and unjustified.

There are two very real hazards caused by this railing where it runs very close to the edge of the bitumen. It is impossible to stop without part of the vehicle being on the road and hazardous to traffic. The authorities must reckon that vehicles don't break down or have flat tyres anymore!

The other concerns kangaroos, particularly at night. Roos will not jump where they cannot see, so they are *channelled* up the road in front of vehicles – a real hazard to them and vehicles. This applies to domestic stock as well. Just another example of excess bureaucracy and the *nanny state* mentality.

LOUD BACKGROUND MUSIC IN TELEVISION PROGRAMS

I can't believe it is just me that has this problem. But if it is as widespread as I suspect, why don't you hear people complain about it?

I know a lot of men, in particular, have trouble hearing at dinner parties, or in rooms full of people. If that is the case, surely the same would apply while watching a film or documentary on TV or in a picture theatre.

I understand that background music is necessary for building the mood, but when it is so loud that you miss half the dialogue, then it is counter-productive.

If there were mass complaints, the powers that be would do something about it, but I am not holding my breath.

I guess that leaves me with three options – put up with the status quo, give up watching TV, or learn to lip read.

12
RIDING THE RATTLER

During the Depression Years, *riding the rattler* (hitching a free ride on trains) was a pretty common pastime. Apparently some police and railway officials turned a blind eye, and others didn't. Back in the 1960's I had a small taste of this desperate pastime, as did a mate of mine only a couple of years ago.

I was pegging the western boundary of the developing Rawlinna Station, with a couple of offsiders. Our camp consisted of a Fordson tractor and four wheel trailer to carry steel posts, stores, water, swags, etc. We had pegged around twenty two kilometres south of the East-West Railway line, which was the northern boundary of Rawlinna. At that time, it was the largest sheep station in the world, covering 12,432 square kilometres. The policy of the company (B.H. MacLachlan Ltd) was to erect its own dingo-proof fence around the station, and I was pegging the western boundary (a distance of one hundred and fifty kilometres), prior to contractors erecting the fence. Work had come to a standstill due to the fact that we had staked a rear tyre on the tractor, with no means to repair it, and not carrying any radio communication in those days, I had decided to walk to a little railway siding called Naretha. It doesn't exist anymore, nor does the lime kiln that operated there for years. It sat literally on the western edge of the Nullarbor Plain. To the west was that part of the South Western Great Victorian Desert, located south of the railway line.

My idea was to walk the twenty two kilometres to Naretha and *ride the rattler* the fifty odd kilometres to the railway town of Rawlinna. I would then ring my mate, Rod Campbell, at the station camp and he would come and pick me up – seemed like a fair plan.

Early next morning I had a good breakfast, made a sandwich or two for lunch, and started walking north of the pegline. It was May, the weather was fine, and there were worse things to be doing. Plenty of wildlife around, and I quite enjoyed the walk. Long before I could see the power lines marking the railway, I heard the *east-bound* passenger express train go through, and some hours later, the *west-bound*. Finally, about four in the afternoon the power lines bobbed up on the horizon, and then the fettlers' houses, shimmering in the mirage.

I approached within half a kilometre of the siding, and finding a small patch of Old Man Saltbush, I made myself comfortable, waiting for the east-bound *fast goods* that I knew would be coming through that evening. I didn't want anyone at the siding or adjacent lime kiln to spot me, not wanting to jeopardize my transport. Many of the Commonwealth railway employees viewed us station blokes with suspicion anyway, and I wasn't taking any chances.

Gradually the sun slipped off the edge of the plain, and dusk arrived. There was a bit of activity around the siding and a quad with a ganger and fettlers arrived back from out along the line. It was completely dark when I heard the *fast goods* approaching from the west, and I moved in closer to the line, lying down behind a stack of old railway sleepers. Soon after, the glaring headlight appeared through the Mulga accompanied by the sound of the big General Motors Diesels. I positioned myself so that I would be about half way along the train when it pulled up. Soon as it did so, I made for the first G.B. (open topped rolling stock) some fifty metres away. I quickly climbed up between it and another van, only to find it was tarped down at the top. Knowing my window of opportunity was small I scrambled down and ran to the next one. As I climbed up, the engine driver sounded the horn, and the train began slowly moving off. No good. This one also was covered with a tarp. I got down quickly and ran alongside the train as it picked up pace. I realised that I only had one more chance and only just managed to grab the ladder and jump up onto the plate. Third time lucky, I thought, but no, it too was covered. I thought briefly about jumping off, but straightaway put that idea out of my head. I was on board and heading east.

I didn't like the idea of sitting on the tarp – not enough to hang on to. So I had no option but to stand on the plate, hanging on tight with both hands to the ladder. I thought it shouldn't be too bad. There was a lot of noise and movement, but I only had to put up with it for an hour or so. Now they call these trains a *fast goods* train, but there is nothing all that fast about them. However, I felt like I was doing a hundred and sixty kilometres an hour. At first I wasn't too bothered, there was no way I was going to go to sleep and lose my grip. But I didn't count on the cold! I hadn't brought a pullover or jacket, thinking I would be inside a 'G.B'. out of the wind. There were usually plenty of empty ones going east. Even though it wasn't mid winter, I soon became very cold. However, it wasn't so much the discomfort, but the fact that I started to lose the feeling in my hands. This was scary, but I had no option but to hang on like a barnacle to a ship bottom.

The time seemed to stand still, made worse by the fact that I couldn't see my watch. After what seemed like all night, I felt the train slowing, and looking around the side of the G.B. I saw the glow of the Rawlinna lights. Eventually the train rolled to a stop. For a second or two I thought my fingers were permanently welded to the rails. When I unattached them, I stepped out on to the good old *Nullarbor* limestone, stamping around the flat to bring a bit of circulation back, thinking there had to be better ways to travel. I was on the north side of the train away from the railway station and limited activity. When the *fast goods* pulled out, I waited until the railway staff had disappeared, walked over to the phone box and surprised Rod with a phone call.

A SHORT RIDE

A mate, Josh, had just finished working on a camel trek operated by Andrew Harper (who purchased the Outback Camel Company from me). He had come in to Alice Springs and intended on travelling down to the Clare Valley to see his mother. However his cheque hadn't come through and he was broke, or didn't have enough for a coach fare. Now Josh is not short of confidence, and it takes a lot to scare him, so he thought why don't I *ride the rattler*, and went around to the railway yards for a look. The Ghan Passenger Train was due to depart that afternoon, and he noticed a few goods vans on the end, including a flat top with a number of motorbikes - on their stands and all roped down.

Sure that he was unobserved, he chucked up his swag and bag and climbed on to the flat top. He had another bag with some tucker and a few cans of beer. He looked forward to a pleasant journey south, intending to get off at Port Augusta. He put his gear in amongst the bikes, and himself also, waiting for the train to depart.

It headed off around 4 pm and as soon as it cleared the built up area, Josh moved out into the open, cracked a can and sat on his swag, enjoying the late afternoon scenery. As the *Ghan* came out of the second gap, Josh was alarmed to see a group of *train spotters*, probably from the Railway Historical Society. Josh ducked back amongst the bikes, uncertain as to whether or not he had been *spotted*. Shortly after, he suspected the worse as the train began losing speed as it approached the crossing of the Stuart Highway near the airport. There were a number of police cars and officers approaching the flat top with drawn revolvers. Josh jumped off the flat top, put his hands on his head and walked toward the approaching officers saying "I surrender".

Several of them grabbed him, and threw him to the ground, holding him there face down. When they had satisfied themselves that he was harmless, and after some robust abuse, they surprisingly told him to get his gear and clear out. It was less than a year since 9/11 in New York, and suspected *terrorists* were flavour of the month. So maybe *riding the rattler* is an activity of the past, it's getting hard to have a *free adventure* these days.

13
PARTIES I HAVE HAD

Patti and I have lived in mostly fairly remote locations for most of our married life. The main criteria I went by when choosing somewhere to live, was whether or not I could operate a camel farm there. That applied to most places, so from there on we could more or less take our pick.

When I was not away running trips, I would be home, mostly staying put for long periods without going out much. It's not that we don't like going out and being with mates, but just that we are very content staying put in the bush and enjoying it.

However it seemed that every ten years on the *big* birthdays, I would have a proper party.

THIRTIETH

I know I had a good big party, but for the life of me I have no recollection of it whatsoever. Must have been a beauty!

FORTIETH

We were on Kangaroo Island living on our farm down in the north-west corner of the island. Firstly, I got a bloke to build me a portable dance floor, and this was installed at a camping ground/barbecue area I had on the other side of the Ravine Creek, from our house. It was a beautiful area under South Australia's tallest trees (literally) sugar gums up to 36 metres high. It was perched above a bush dam. I organised a DJ from Kingscote, a couple of kegs, while Patti organised the tucker for sixty people.

It's not easy getting people to visit an Island just for a short party, so I said it was for a weekend, or longer if they chose to stay on.

The Ravine was just about the most remote location possible on Kangaroo Island and transport had to be organised for the majority of people who were not driving, but flying to Kingscote, one hundred kilometres away. I cleaned up the old Commer camel truck, and went in to pick them up, late on the Saturday morning. I had bales of hay around the edges of the crate, and there were some *interested* looks and comments. Over forty people and their swags etc climbed up into the back of the camel truck, much to the amazement of some of the many *conventional* travellers, and we headed off for the *Ravine*. They all enjoyed it so much, I thought about charging them!

Things got under way about three o'clock, with some music, and a bit of *live entertainment* such as recitals and acts, soap box, etc. Then the eating bit, with much of the meat comprising of wallaby rissoles, a specialty of Patti's. The reader will be left wondering how this very common protected species ended up in rissoles, the only thing I'll say is that I didn't shoot them.

Around about eight o'clock, I noticed a suspicious gathering of a group of blokes, who soon after, moved quickly towards me. Before I could shin up a sugar gum (impossible anyway) they grabbed me, and forcibly placed me into what to all intents and purposes, was a coffin!

I was then carried down to the dam, and felt myself sailing through the air before a thud/splash (the bloody coffin wasn't padded). I then felt myself floating blissfully on the water. I was almost certain I hadn't *passed away*, although one can never be sure. I knocked the top off my *coffin* and paddled into shore, apparently performing an *item* that wasn't on my list of *items*.

After that the show settled down to dancing, with the new floor standing up (not literally) very well. Sometime before breakfast I found myself in a swag.

Later in the morning after some kind of breakfast, the whole show began a move to *Harvey's Return,* our local beach. This was located just a few kilometres down the road from our place, and is a delightful little cove, which only has a small beach in summer. It is practically always deserted. Remains of an old mini railway line goes down the very steep track to a large rock base that used to have a derrick on it – for unloading supplies for Cape Borda Lighthouse nearby. A draught horse would activate a turntable to haul the single rail vehicle up and down. Quite an operation.

Getting down to the beach (the day was 35 degrees) probably resembled activity on the Ho Chi Minh trail. The new keg was slung under a mallee rail with two slaves staggering along under the weight. All the lunch food had to be carried down as well, and a lot of hangovers must have been not improving.

A very pleasant afternoon was had on the beach and in the sea, before dragging ourselves back up the cliff and onto the camel truck. I then drove the bulk of them back to Kingscote airport, and by the time I returned home I was definitely ready for bed.

A few stragglers had taken up the offer to stay on, and finally after a week, the only partygoer left was my old mate, BJ Elliot. He left the next morning, and I said to Patti, "I'm going up the top paddock to put in a strainer post!" Now here's the thing – I was only away for an hour before I was home again. Patti asked me why I was back, and I couldn't give her a proper answer. I just didn't feel like digging a hole, or anything else for that matter. I was like it for weeks, and someone finally diagnosed it as *male menopause.* Pretty scary. That's one good reason why I only have a proper party every ten years.

FIFTIETH

By this time we are living up at *the Range* in the hills above McLaren Flat. This was to be a two stage party – a sort of open day on the Saturday with people dropping in and out as they saw fit.

It was a lazy sort of party really (some would say normal) with people sitting around drinking grog, eating, and yarning. Very pleasant with the temperature around thirty degrees. Apart from a few long distance guests the show was over by Sunday breakfast.

The second stage took place a week later on the good old Murray River, a bit upstream of where we now live. We were soon to be moving up here to live and I had a 9 x 6 metre pontoon ready for a landing. It was moored upstream at Markaranka. Around fourteen of us drove up and hopped on the pontoon, with swags and overnight clothes only. All the blokes wore dress shirts and ties (ridiculous!) and whatever they liked below that, and the girls in similar mode. They all probably wondered about the lack of grog and tucker (apart from an esky that had one drink per person in it) but were too polite, or knowledgeable to say anything about it. A table down the middle with tablecloth and place settings. Everyone brought their own chairs.

We were underway about four pm, and about an hour later a speedboat could be seen approaching from the direction of Morgan. It pulled up alongside, and one of the Morgan publicans began unloading eskies full of seafood etc, and enough grog to do the job. Looks of relief were observed on several of the assembled.

As the sun went down we were on to our sweets, and it was only then that I realised we had forgotten the coffee. Not good, especially for the next morning. It was a moonless night as we drifted coffee-less on a three kilometre an hour current.

After a while we spotted the lights of a houseboat, moored on the southern bank. Salvation, I thought. With a little bit of manual paddling we aligned the flight path of our vessel with that of the stationary object and waited. We hit the small houseboat with a loud *thud*, which caused a shriek to emanate from the houseboat. "Excuse me", I said, "Is there any chance of trading a jar of coffee for a cask of red?" The only answer to that was the sound of doors being locked and the lights going out. No matter what we said (we said a lot), not a sound or movement came from the boat. It was probably a young couple on their honeymoon, but this was their worst nightmare!

After a while we gave up. Short of storming the vessel, there was no way we were getting coffee or anything else from this houseboat. I realised that our general approach had probably lacked a bit of subtlety. We drifted on, coffee-less.

At some stage we rolled the swags out alongside, and under the table, called it a day. The end of half a century for me – so far the trip have been very enjoyable.

The next thing we all knew (well, most of us) was when there was a great CRASH, and at the same time something hard was pushing into my short ribs from outside of my swag. A couple of torches were switched on, and it appeared that we had drifted into a huge dead tree, lying in the river. We were going nowhere, so after a few varied comments all again became horizontal.

I was awakened some hours later by a pair of galahs screeching abuse from the top branch of the dead red gum. Fair enough, I thought, they probably had a nest somewhere in this dead *nature's boarding house.*

All in sundry gradually got mobile, and got off for a walk around. No habitation in sight, which was good and we got a fire going and cooked up a pile of eggs and bacon – but no coffee, or tea for that matter. I get sick of houseboats sometimes, but I would have been glad to see one this morning.

After a bit of manual labour, we got under way again, and about lunch time arrived at Nikalapko station where a couple of vehicles had been delivered. So much for my fiftieth.

SIXTIETH

This one was held down at *White Hill Farm,* organised largely by my old mate, the late Bill Oliver. More of a conventional sort of do, held in the complex that Sue Oliver now operates a very successful wedding reception enterprise from. We had a band organised by an old mate, Richard Gryst, and dancing was the go. I had a few prizes for various things, of which a Rooster, was one. I hope he went to a loving home

A nice lazy morning next morning, and another milestone was notched up.

SEVENTIETH

Shit, I thought, that didn't take long. Seems like only last year I was having my sixtieth, but sure enough calendars don't lie.

A hundred people were spending the night at the *Camel Farm* at Weston Flat, and I had a lot of campsites worked out with numbers, in the mallee scrub along the cliffs. The *swaghouse* was the venue. This consists of roofed, open area with a raised jarrah floor, located thirty metres form the edge of sheer cliffs. Not an ideal place for a party some would say, and they could have a point. But most of the crew were not teenagers, and I did string a rope from tree to tree near the cliff edge, with a no go area beyond that. I'm a great believer in people being responsible for their own safety.

Most of the people were on the site by four o'clock, and the temperature was around twenty seven degrees. Couldn't be better. At precisely five o'clock a bright red aircraft flew low over head, and the assembled suffered a severe flour bombing, but the *bombardier* was still doing her apprenticeship, and there were no *whiteouts.* Bits and pieces of a very good Adelaide band called *Midnight Martini* began to arrive, at about the same time as the Hahn Family (Neville, Craig and Nicole) began setting up their very professional bush catering operation. It consisted of a saltbush mutton wether on a spit with hot veg (Hors d'oeuvres was local sushi provided by Hayashi from the Waikerie United Service Station, which is a bit more than just a service station.) Sweets consisted of apple pie and cream from the excellent Waikerie Bakery, so malnutrition was not going to be a problem.

The night's entertainment was varied, with one of the earlier acts choreographed by my ex Circus Oz daughter Katherine and two of eldest daughter Georgi's youngest, Solomon and Kale. Some acrobatics. The usual *soapbox* and other acts, plus the dancing.

A mate Owen Davies was present with his excellent pet dingo, who was taken around and introduced to all in sundry.

Next morning with most of the crowd still present, Georgi and Katherine read out a poem they had composed about their old man, which brought a tear to the eye. Last but not least, Jimmy Ellis appeared out of the scrub and gave a very good impression of Rolf Harris' *Jake the Peg.* How many blokes do you know with one eye and three legs?

14
THE PAPRIKA CLUB

For many years, from probably around the late 1950's well up into the 1970's, there was a night club in Adelaide's Hindley Street called the Paprika Club. It was a fair dinkum night club unlike many of today's efforts, with a very good live band, compere/singer and a very well endowed female performer who went by the name of *Big Pretzel.* Appreciating good music, I would visit this place irregularly when I had the time off from the sheep stations and later the safaris, with plenty of money in my pocket – a very *definite pre-requisite.*

On one such occasion, a group of us decided to have a night out. There was Patti and myself (before we were married), David Brook from Birdsville with his lady, a geologist mate of mine called Haggis Shackleton with his first wife, a Chinese lady called Mae, and a Fijian/ Ellis islander called Joe Hatch and his Fijian/Chinese wife, Marianne. It was at the period just before B.Y.O. arrived in South Australia, and because of this I saw a chance to reduce our wine bill drastically. Born and bred in McLaren Vale, I always resented paying the exorbitant prices for wine that the club charged.

With this in mind, a few days before this outing, I phoned the club, and asked details of their wine list, noting that it contained Hardy's St. Thomas

Burgundy, and Old Castle Riesling, a pair of tried and proven *plonks*. I then went to Hardy's cellar door at McLaren Vale where I was well known, and purchased half a dozen bottles of each, at very reasonable rates. When we met up in Adelaide on the Saturday night, I had this dozen, in two airways bags. Fortunately, the night was cold and wet, and myself and one of the other blokes were able to wear overcoats into the club. Probably wouldn't have bothered under normal circumstances, but the thing was, we had to conceal the airways bags. We adjusted the carry straps so that the bags hung level with our knees, and were hidden by the coats. When we went into the restaurant, the two of us in particular, made a bee-line smartly for our booked table (I knew the number), sitting down before the very attentive, efficient and suave Estonian maitre de could take and hang our coats up. As soon as we sat down, we had it organized so that we undid buckles and placed the bags under the table, hidden by the long white table-cloths. We then let the man have our overcoats. So far, so good, we reckoned.

First thing, we ordered a bottle of St Thomas Burgundy and another of Old Castle Riesling, from the small, arrogant, feisty Italian drink waiter - another man very efficient at his job. Unfortunately, there was no way around this for our little scheme to work. We wasted no time in emptying these bottles, and waiting until the staff were absent, quickly pulled the empty bottles from the wine buckets, replacing them with two opened full ones.

Almost straight away, the Italian wine waiter swooped on our table like an attacking Peregrine Falcon. With a fluid gesture he went to pluck a perceived empty bottle from the bucket, and bloody near dislocated his shoulder, as well as slopping some red wine on the immaculate table-cloth. He gawked at the full bottle like Manuel from Faulty Towers T.V. series, his face registering disbelief, then rage. He verbally raked us with a burst of Italian as we sat back in all innocence. His professional dignity had been *dealt a cruel blow* and he was livid. Clutching the bottle, he stalked across the room like a revved up Bantam rooster, and pulled up in front of *Mr. Cool,* the Estonian maitre de, looking up at him and shaking the offending bottle, and shooting off another burst of Italian. The maitre de looked down at him with an icy superior look, one eyebrow slightly raised. The drink waiter scuttled off to the scullery to repair his loss of face, while *Mr. Cool,* holding the offending bottle between thumbs and forefinger, like an illegal immigrant (which you could argue, it was!) navigated his way through the tables in our direction - a man to be reckoned with.

The floor show hadn't yet started, but by the looks on the faces of the surrounding throng, it was going to run a poor second to this little performance. *Mr. Cool* cruised to a halt at our table, placing the bottle of *St Thomas* on the middle of the table. Looking distastefully at the wine stains on the table-cloth, his opening enquiry sort of meant *what the bloody hell is going on here??* Here was a man to be taken seriously, and judging by the looks directed at me, I was to be the elected spokesman.

One of my dubious talents is that I am able to maintain a straight face in this sort of situation, while at the same time, dispensing a line of verbal rubbish relevant to the situation required – if you know what I mean. "Look mate", I said, "we seem to have upset your bloke", nodding in the direction of the kitchen. "I don't know why", I continued, carefully avoiding the faces of my mates, "we are from the west, and are just doing the B.Y.O. thing, can't understand what got into the man. Something's obviously upset him." The maitre de gave me a penetrating stare that left us all under no illusions, that he wasn't aware of our little game. Then he replied in perfect accented English "I apologize for the misunderstanding Sir. Your B.Y.O is acceptable, and our corkage rate will be two dollars fifty per bottle. Enjoy your evening Sir". With that, he executed a perfect three hundred and sixty degree turn, and glided through the assembled diners, and out of sight into the kitchen. Trying to keep our faces in earnest mode, we discussed the development. Our little effort had been partially successful, but the maitre de had responded with a massive two dollars fifty corkage fee. Anyway it still resulted in a very large saving in the beverage department for the evening.

If we thought that was the end of the night's drama, we were wrong. As the evening progressed, so did our wine consumption. We were halfway through our main course, when Mae suddenly threw up (big time). Now this in itself is always unfortunate and embarrassing for all concerned, particularly the *thrower upper*. The extra drama was due to the fact that the man in charge of the clean-up was none other than our friend, the Italian waiter. He was obviously given instructions by *Mr. Cool,* who was standing as far away as it was possible to be, from our table. The Italian approached us like a game cock on steroids, and *our table* sat like statues, avoiding each others' gaze, as he began the clean up.

For myself, I wasn't game to move or speak. These days you are more likely to get a stiletto in your ribs in Hindley Street than you were back then, but my natural caution warned me that one false move or comment right then could very likely result in just that scenario. He had to remove all the gear off the table, including our half eaten main courses (they went back to the kitchen for heating up, so as always, I gave the *Paprika* full marks for professionalism). He mopped the table, brought out a fresh cloth, re-set it, and brought back our meals. And so the night went on, memorable by any standards.

Footnote: I never ever attempted to B.Y.O. grog to that place again, and all future bookings were made in someone else's name.

There was one other event, worth relating, that occurred at the Paprika a few years later. Patti and I were dining out there with a N.T. cattleman mate, Roy Driver, and a girlfriend. Roy was in Adelaide attending a cattle sale where a lot of Elkedra Station cattle were sold, for very good prices.

During the evening, Roy and I went off to the gents toilet at the same time. It appeared empty of other inhabitants, and I chose that moment to insist that I paid for the wine that night. (Roy had previously insisted that he would pick up the whole tab). We were in the process of arguing about this matter, when a muffled voice from an occupied cubicle muttered "If you blokes are pretty right, how about slipping me a spin under the door – I'm a bit short!" And we did!

15
TASMANIAN SAFARI

I had been to Tasmania previously on a family trip with Patti and the kids, but had never operated down there commercially. I had a trout fishing mate and we had stayed with him at his shack in the central lakes district. On that occasion I had really wanted to see what was the highest hardwood tree in the world (it alternated with one in the Dandenong Ranges in Victoria, depending on high winds knocking the tops off either at different times) which was a Mountain Ash (*Eucalyptus regans*).

I made enquiries everywhere to no avail. No one had a clue what I was on about, until I struck a forestry bloke who knew about it. He gave me the location, and I made plans to visit it. However, the night before a storm had blown a large tree over the track that led to it, and I missed out. Didn't have the right vehicle or a chainsaw.

In November 2002, we drove the Oka on to the *Spirit of Tasmania* at Port Melbourne. On board were Patti, my mate Bill Oliver, and old clients Eileen Nelson and Glenda Benners.

The main idea of this little trip was to get in to the forestry areas where the public were forbidden to go, and get an idea of what was really happening. The clearing of old growth forests had long occupied my mind.

As we drove on to the vehicle deck, all vehicles were pulled up, and a lady checked my vehicle for bombs. Only took a couple of minutes, and I was glad I didn't have shares in the Spirit of Tasmania.

We drove off on to the Island State. This short trip was to be a *smorgasboard* of experiences, and observations. Camping in Tasmania is a bit like Russian roulette when it comes to the weather. I was carrying swags, but were prepared to get under some sort of a roof every now and then if it rained too much.

An early stop was the Arthur River on the west coast. Did a trip in a large motor cruiser with skipper Robert and Bridie his offsider. Up close and personal with a pair of White Bellied sea eagles. The female was apparently forty seven years old, and had been using the current nest (in a large tree near the river) for thirty eight years. Her first mate had been killed and she was re-mated with a younger male. They were used to being hand fed with fish from the boat and that is always entertaining.

Plenty of bubbles indicating platypus, but no animals sighted. We went on a very good bush walk with this couple which was very well interpreted, especially the botany.

Lots of interesting meetings with locals. Eileen recorded this conversation with a young bloke at a raspberry farm where we pulled up. He said to me "Hey, where did you guys come from?" I explained, and then asked "How far to Lake Peddar?" Young bloke said "Dunno, never been there. Dad went once and got a *peddar penny,* before they changed it". I then said "What's this river called?" Young bloke – "No idea". Rex, "Er, where's the nearest fuel station?" Young bloke – "Haven't got a clue". However he was cheerful and friendly, and sold excellent raspberries.

Over to Bruny Island, and had no trouble in finding that tiny Tasmanian endemic bird, the Forty Spotted Pardalote.

A nice camp at Stumpy Bay, without rain. Plenty of wallabies, but a very vocal endemic Yellow Wattlebird kept us awake half the night.

Drove through the *Styx* forest region and shuddered at the huge areas of clear felled forest. The more you see of Australian Government policy on forestry in old growth forest, the more you wonder at the stupidity of it all. In Tasmania, particularly, it is mainly subsidised by the State Government to provide jobs. It does that but ignores the fact that in the long run far more sustainable jobs will be created by Tourism, not to mention the overall health of the environment. Australia wide, plantation forestry is more than enough to supply the wood chipping industry. We stand to lose two parrot species in the future, the Orange Bellied and Swift parrot, the world's fastest parrot. Both rely on old growth forest in Tasmania to breed. The Orange Bellied Parrot (less than a hundred birds in the wild) looks unsaveable, but it is crucial that nesting areas used by the Swift parrot are undisturbed.

Several of our camps were in off limit areas, just to see what goes on behind the impressive façade of forest bordering on the main Highways, and it would break your heart to see it.

I was very keen to see a Tiger Quoll, and we would regularly collect road kill, and leave it near our campsites. On one night when we were camped in a forestry area in heavy rain, we put a spotlight on a dead wallaby, and a shadowy animal about the size and shape of a Tiger Quoll was sin attendance, but couldn't say for sure.

Saw plenty of Tasmanian Devils, but this was well before the disastrous disease that has decimated their ranks.

We did a very nice boat trip on the Pieman River, on a beautiful fifty foot huon pine motor cruiser. There was only our party and a honeymoon couple that were oblivious to absolutely everything except themselves. The skipper was called John. We got going and he started off giving this rambling oratory. He sounded so uncomfortable that I went up and put him out of his misery. I told him *I was in the business*, and not to worry about the spiel. In the end we came up and sat next to him and had a good yarn as we travelled, much to his great relief. He knew his stuff, and turned out he was an ex fisherman. Later it began raining. That night we were due to head toward Straun and I asked him if he knew of an old shed or somewhere we could keep dry. He said, "Yeah, I do – my place". Seemed he had a shed in his back yard, and said we were welcome to camp there.

Later that afternoon we located his house on the edge of Straun in the teeming rain, and he installed us in his shed. It was more like a museum, with several old wooden boats, and masses of fishery paraphernalia. We managed to find space for five swags, and he brought a small barbecue down and installed it. It was a hilarious, entertaining and educational night. He had been a professional fisherman for years, and had given it away recently. Not because he wanted to, but because he was so disgusted by particularly the practice of net scraping the bottom where virtually nothing escapes. He said there were whole areas denuded of practically all life. There was a large trunk that he opened up, full of a variety of deep sea coral that he had brought back.

Soon it was time to drive back on to the Spirit of Tasmania, all of us quite a bit more knowledgeable than when we had driven off.

16
BOATS DOWN THE BULLOO

The Bulloo River is a unique system located on the eastern edge of the Sturt Stoney Desert in Queensland – sandwiched between the Murray/Darling and Lake Eyre Basins. It is a *closed catchment* off low ranges, causing it to fall quickly. Unless your timing is right, you don't *miss the boat,* you miss the river!

For a number of years I have been waiting for an opportunity to run a boat safari down it. In 2010 and 2011 it did run, but I was otherwise occupied on the Warburton and Cooper rivers.

I have a mate called Dogger Dare who lives in Thargomindah. He keeps an eye on the Bulloo and Paroo rivers, and contacts me if they are *suitable* for a trip. In this case I had a bit over a week to find a party and get going.

For these *one off/slightly hazardous* type of trips, I usually invite people along who I reckon could put up with *whatever comes along,* but being a commercial operator, this can't always apply. However, on this occasion I certainly had the right party, seven people including a journalist from the Outback magazine.

There was Brenton Hicks, a farmer and an old mate and client who likes to take his kayak – a very good man for these trips, no fear, always cheerful and physically fit. Mike Arnold from Waikerie, he owns a fruit block, and has been captain of the Waikerie CFS (fire service) forever - over seventy but tough and physically fit. Edith Martens, a homeopath from the Adelaide Hills in her 60's and very fit. Richard McEvoy, in his 60's, fit enough and a very keen photographer. Rocky Powell, an Adelaide banker around sixty, and fit enough. Ann Pye, ex station girl from the Territory who had a law degree, and works in Alice Springs in a Government Department responsible for water. A keen botanist. Emma Mulholland was the journo from the Outback magazine, late twenties, and as it proved quite unflappable.

So it was that on February 7th 2012, Rick Moore and I set off with two vehicles and a party of seven (nine in all). Brenton Hicks, one of my regulars was bringing his kayak as he had done on past trips.

The Bulloo has never had boats down it, and there was much excitement in the party. We drove to Broken Hill where we had two more people and Brenton to pick up including, Emma Mulholland.

After a night at Christine Hugo's excellent Lodge Motel, where I usually stay, we headed north through Tibbooburra, Noccundra and Eromanga to Quilpie, which sits just below the headwaters of the Bulloo. Some excellent local help saw us set up camp below the town bridge. The river here was around thirty to forty metres wide, and flowing at about six kilometres an hour. The inland had been experiencing a couple of weeks of unusually mild weather, with the maximum temperatures were between 28 – 35 degrees. Very few flies, (surprising) but a few sandflies and mossies.

Next morning we headed off around nine thirty am, me in front, Brenton in his kayak in the middle and Rick bringing up the rear. We had UHF radio communication between the boats.

The river maintained its average width of thirty metres with quite a lot of snags and trees (River Red Gum, Coolibah, River Cooba, and Ti Tree) in the river itself. It is to be expected on these types of rivers, and we are used to dealing with it. The course was particularly meandering with lovely riverine scenery. However, when you are operating a boat under these circumstances, you don't have much chance to enjoy the scenery. You come around a bend, and process what is in front of you. If snags or trees in the river look to be a problem I slow my boat and study the scene. Very often, I will *do a uee* and come around for another look. There is usually an option or two for negotiating a *Kelly's wood yard* situation, and it's just a matter of picking the most promising.

I will then go through, and if *clear sailing* I give the second boat the all clear, or maybe suggest an alternative. In this case we rarely went longer than ten minutes between *Kelly's wood yard*' situations.

We had travelled some twelve kilometres when I weaved through a couple of dead trees and rounded a tight bend, with Rick about fifty metres behind me. Suddenly I had an urgent signal from Rick to Stop, so I turned and headed back into the current around the bend. The sight we were presented with definitely meant we wouldn't be travelling anymore on this particular day. Rick's boat had *gone in*. The left hand rear of the steel canopy frame was caught around a dead branch, with the front of the boat under water. People were standing up, looking a bit startled, while various items of *cargo* were beginning to float downstream towards my boat. The beauty of these tinnies is that due to the flotation inside the seats, they cannot sink, so part of our pre-trip instructions centre around holding on to the boat if such a situation as this should occur. Then, wait for instructions while the staff rectify the situation. The people did just that. Unfortunately the same thing couldn't be said for the gear, as we watched loaves of bread, cans of beer, cabbages, etc. float past our boat.

I went onto shore with my boat, and unloaded my people. From there it was only about ten metres to Rick's boat so we tossed over a rope and secured it to the shore.

We helped one person to the shore. Then I noticed Ann, swimming along firmly attached to her swag. It actually was her swag in this case, so I suppose she had an extra vested interest in making sure she kept hold of it. She was making her way toward the bank with a steely determination, and I stepped into the river and helped her and her swag ashore. Swags in particular, mainly due to the foam mattress become extremely heavy when dunked in a river, but fortunately they float.

I then headed down river in my boat with a couple of people to begin collecting our gear, or most of it. I went about four hundred metres before I reckoned I was around the head of it, and we began collecting items. All of the personal bags had been tied in and most of the swags. Half way back up river we encountered Brenton floating down stream (not in his kayak!) securing a few items in the forks of trees. He thrives on drama, and is very good in these types of situations. In twenty minutes we were back to the scene of the action. Rick and Rocky were still in the boat securing gear. The next couple of hours were taken up with ferrying all of the gear to a camp I had established on the western bank. Fortunately it was one of the rare dry spots that we had encountered so far (our earlier smoko camp which had been up a slippery bank standing in boggy ground amongst large clumps of grass). Only problem was, it was on top of a three metre, very steep wet bank, and getting people and heavy gear up was challenging. By about one o'clock we had all gear up, with swags opened up for drying, and wet bags emptied out. We boiled the billy and had a well-earned lunch.

Much of the afternoon was taken up with getting the submerged outboard running again, which it finally did. We rely on these Yamaha outboards so totally in remote situations, and our faith is never misplaced. We also hauled the boat to the other bank and bailed it out, and by late afternoon we were all set to tackle the river again.

Next morning we awoke to a nasty shock. The river had dropped a metre, which is what happens to these small catchment rivers, but thought we had more time available to us. We got underway by 8am, with a reduced flow in the river. There were more snags showing but most of them didn't bother us too much. Several times I had to get my boat in a position in order to cut through branches with my handsaw, to enable us to get through. Sometimes I would do it from my position in the rear and sometimes a front passenger would do it. All good exercise.

Twice that morning, Eastern and then Western Grey kangaroos swam the river in front of our boats. It's not often that I have seen this, so was a big highlight for people.

Bird numbers and variety was disappointing, but not surprising with practically all of inland Australia looking like a garden. Brolgas and Red tailed Black Cockatoos had been seen.

On the first day we had pulled ourselves over a submerged fence, but we now came across a flood gate that blocked our passage. Flood gates consist of a cable crossing the river as part of a fence line. Usually light fence or netting is suspended from these.

In dry times it keeps stock from going through, but is designed so as to be expendable when floods can often carry it away. It saves the expense of replacing expensive and labour intensive fencing. As this country used to be predominantly sheep we could expect more of these flood gates to negotiate.

In this one and a few others we cut out sections, just big enough to enable our boats to pass through, but easily patched when repairs were done after the flood had subsided.

Smoko and lunch were both in pleasant scenic situations. Both of these daily stops are keenly anticipated by all of the party. We carry thermoses of tea and coffee for smoko, but boil the billy for lunch. Our *ten minute smoko* is always around half an hour, and lunch is an hour on most occasions.

We had some relatively open *reaches*, of up to half a kilometre long, and kept making pretty good time. A number of tricky situations with trees and snags, requiring quick action on the tiller, and more cutting with the saws.

My hope was to catch up with the flood, but so far there was no sign of it. I had phoned a new contact of mine in Quilpie called *Wog*, and ordered replacement stores for the ones that we had lost. He was going to deliver them to Pinkanellie Station, one of only two homesteads we would see on the river between Quilpie and Thargomindah.

Around four o'clock we came to a raised concrete causeway which got the Thargomindah – Quilpie road across the river. The water was only 10 centimetres over the causeway, and it took us over half an hour to literally drag both loaded boats across and into water on the other side. All day long we could see the river was continuing to drop.

A few times we came across red stony patches of the Sturt Stoney Desert, a welcome variety to the wall to wall gums and high banks. With it though, came shallow water and rocks, so there was plenty of getting out of boats and pushing. Once we passed a wild pig carcass, hanging high in a tree.

We carried on through thick strands of Ti Tree, attractive, but always a worry with fast water. A little bit of *gardening* got us through. We reached a point five kilometres between the crossing and camped at seven o'clock. A big day of around a hundred kilometres travelled – river kilometres that is. This river had more bends than any I had been on.

I was able to find a nice high dry camp, once we waded through about ten metres of glutinous mud. It was on a long island with nice views all around. We were using insect domes, which we do on summer trips due to the usual hordes of mosquitoes, although for some reason they were hardly needed on this occasion. The mossies really were not too bad at all.

Next morning, to our concern, the river had dropped yet another metre. This was not looking good. My main fear was running out of navigable water, and not being able to get our vehicles in to pull us out. Most of the flood plain was sodden, and in all probability a helicopter would be required to get people and minimal gear out to where vehicles could drive. The boats would have to be left for the time being. Not a situation I looked forward to.

We were off before eight, but straight away we were touching the bottom in some places. A couple of kilometres further on, we negotiated another flood gate. After more running aground I decided to *pull the plug*, as the river had done. We turned around and began heading back up river. Very disappointing, but really no viable alternative.

Things were really hard going. Fast running shallow water, much of it over rocks, and much of our time was out of the boats.

We had smoko on a high bank amongst a high profuse tussock grass, and continued on our laborious way. On occasions we would have to have all hands on one boat at a time, pulling and pushing them through shallow water.

Finally, about midday, the causeway came in sight, much to our relief. I had a walk around and found a possible camp out of the mud under a large shady Coolibah, and we had lunch there.

I phoned Dogger, and he said he could bring our vehicles back, with Robin, his wife, and a mate. Probably next day. I then rang Wog, and fortunately he hadn't yet taken our stores down to Pinkanellie, so he said he would drop them off tomorrow, on his way to Thargomindah. Mailman was one of his jobs.

We had a relaxing afternoon fishing and yabbying (no luck) and swimming. A few vehicles went past, most of them very surprised to see the boats next to the causeway.

Wog came next day with our stores, and an hour or so later Dogger arrived. He helped us get loaded up, and accompanied us into Quilpie. It was good to catch up with Dogger again. He had been a great help to us in our Paroo river trip back in March 2000 (*'Boats in the Desert'*).

We fuelled up at Wog's fuel depot. Quilpie was a good experience, and typical of these western Queensland towns. Full of characters and the Australian spirit. Friendly people and nothing too much trouble.

Headed off mid afternoon, for the Cooper channels, where we camped that night. We would spend the next couple of days at Innamincka and Coongie Lakes, before heading down the Strzelecki track to the Flinders and home.

The Bulloo River was a unique experience, shorter than anticipated, (we had travelled 120 kilometres out of an approximate 400 *river* kilometres to Thargomindah – below Thargomindah the river soon split into channels, before running into a large *floodout*) but very enjoyable and interesting. Our party of myself and Rick, Brenton Hicks, Rocky Page, Richard McEvoy, Ann Pye, Edith Martens, Mick Arnold and Emma Mulholland, had been a happy, gutsy and cohesive group.

17
THREE RIVERS SAFARI

This was supposed to be a trip down the Murrumbidgee River from Hay to the junction with the Murray, and down the Murray to the Boundary Bend or Euston. But it didn't turn out that way.

Peter Young and I were the *boaties* and we had a party of three ladies (Joan Brown, Lizzie Crisp and Janet Atkins). Using one of my fourteen foot tinnies and towing a Zodiac inflatable, we stopped at Balranald to drop some fuel off at the caravan park, which is right on the river.

During our usual check on the trailer, we noticed the hitch had broken and it was hanging on the safety chains. If it had to happen, it couldn't have been at a better place. Right opposite the park, was a bloke with an extremely well set up workshop. Peter and I went over and knocked on the front door. The bloke (Dave) wasn't home but his wife (Janis) was, and she told us to *help ourselves* to the facilities, which was very kind of her. In an hour Peter had knocked up a strengthened replacement, and we were back in business.

Arrived in Hay around dusk and drove fifteen kilometres back down the north side of the river to the Hay Weir. We rang our contact man in Hay

(Jim Bisset) and arranged to meet him next morning to organise getting the Oka down to our finish point.

Jim and his wife Beryl live on a backwater of the Murrumbidgee in this quite remarkable *house*. It is a long corrugated iron, steel frame series of round roof shed-like structures. A family show. Besides Jim and Beryl, a son and daughter in law, are in one section and three grandchildren share the other section. There are upstairs areas. A common verandah overlooks the river. Very comfortable and suited to the climate.

During *smoko*, Jim mentioned that the Lachlan River was still very high, higher than it had been for many years. I thought that here was an opportunity not to be missed. We will swap the Murrumbidgee for the Lachlan. Half an hour later we were on the road heading for the town of Hillston on the Lachlan, two hours away. We had Jim with us, to bring the Oka and trailer back to Hay.

On the way we had a look at the old One Tree Hotel, which has been de-licensed for many years. The owners had spent a lot of money restoring the native pine building. Then through the little town of Booligal to call into Eurugabah Station. Jenny Scheaffer was very admiring of our party of ladies, saying that her idea of camping out was on the tenth floor of the Hilton with the window open! Had a check of the river there which was narrow with a fair bit of timber growing in the channel.

After calling on her husband Bill, trucking cattle further on, we drove on to Hillston, a thriving little town. There is a weir a few kilometres downstream, so we drove down below it to put in the boats.

After lunch, we loaded up, us down the river and Jim back to Hay in the Oka. It was my intention to try and make it through to the junction with the Murrumbidgee, between Hay and Balranald. There was a very large swamp below the town of Oxley that could prove a challenge. We had the frame and canopy off this time due to the expected low branches. One of the girls was sitting in the Zodiac. The current was running at about three kilometres an hour with the channel averaging from thirty to fifty metres wide. Thick Red Gum, Black Box and some River Cooba on the banks.

We did an hour and a quarter to 4:30pm and made what was to be our best camp for the Lachlan. High and dry on a bend.

Joan found a White-winged Chough's nest in a tree above her swag. Very interesting bird. They get around in flocks from one to two dozen birds, building several large mud nests, over half as big as a Magpie Larks (Peewee). Sexes are pretty much indistinguishable. They have a series of regular feeding spots in their area, visiting each of them every day. The group stick to themselves, but to keep the gene pool healthy, young birds are *kidnapped'* from one group to the other. Black birds slightly smaller than a magpie, with broad white wing patches and red eyes.

Away by 8:30 next morning. Birdlife was steadily improving, four species of duck, with lots of Grey Teal and ducklings. Plenty of *obstructions* on the river, natural and man-made. Had to cut our way through several sections, then around a tight bend and we are confronted with a footbridge across the river! There was a homestead on the banks obscured by vegetation, with a dog going berserk, probably on a chain. Just managed to get onto the bank, then ease our way under the bridge, with centimetres of head clearance. Totally illegal I would reckon, but navigation not important anymore. River very convoluted, but full of interest, with *character* River Gums of all shapes and sizes. Quite a few wild goats of varying colours.

Then a low road bridge which we were expecting. Peter had his lap top computer set up, equipped with mapping software, so we were pre-warned with most development, obstructive or otherwise. We were passing a number of homesteads, but saw no people. The only boat of any kind visible was one old tinny, leaning up against a pump shed. Odd cotton fields visible, but ran out of them after a while. The water was mostly around 30 centimetres below the banks. A pleasant lunch by a huge gum growing in prostrate forms out of the river, then on again. A couple of wild pigs were seen amongst the mass of green growth either side of the river. Like the most of the rest of Australia this country has had exceptional rains.

That night we had a *camp of convenience* on a damp flat, most of the country being water-logged.

Away by quarter to eight next day. Straight away, heaps more of everything including birdlife, sheep, cattle, goats, pigs and hundreds of Eastern Grey kangaroos. Never seen so many roos from a river. On two occasions, roos swam the river in front of us. Saw three or four foxes, all very healthy.

Things were looking up in the raptor department as well, with a Swamp Harrier and two Peregrine Falcons. Then, suddenly a Goshawk appeared in front of us chasing a Nankeen Night Heron, a bird four times its size. I don't think it was serious, but the Heron was taking dramatic evasive action.

Constantly there were Grey Teal with very large broods of ducklings. They would do their convincing broken wing act in front of the boat, as the tiny ducklings zipped across the surface, their feet going like eggbeaters, before diving under the surface. Numerous pairs and small flocks of Black Duck as well. Very pleasing, as they took a big hit in the last drought. As did Straw Necked Ibis, but we were seeing them in big numbers down this river.

White Necked Herons were very common, and once the tiny brilliant blue of an azure King Fisher. Saw an immature White Bellied Sea Eagle which was *bird of the day*.

This was the sort of day that makes inland river boating special.

Around mid-afternoon we came to the junction of the Lachlan and another creek, an anabranch. Our local information was that this anabranch should be a lot clearer travelling with less timber in the river. It very soon became clear that we were *up shit creek without a paddle*.

Pulling over logs and cutting through Red Gum, we gave it away after an hour or so, having travelled a couple of kilometres. Reversed our route back to the junction, by this time it was almost dark, with nothing each side but swampland. Finally found some sort of a camp at the junction, with a little bit of soggy ground surrounded by bog. Got a good fire going, then, Peter found an area of dry ground nearby, so we carried our swags over there for the night. Rain was forecast for the next day.

In the morning, a bit of drizzle, so we got busy and erected the *hootchie* (large tarp) and made ourselves comfortable for the day, with a large fire out the front.

About nine, Peter and I headed off in the boat, along the main channel of the Lachlan that was now only ten to fifteen metres wide and full of timber. A lot of cutting, and then areas of good going, lasting almost half a kilometre on occasions. We were heading for a track shown on the map that let us exit the river without heading fifty kilometres back to Ulonga Station. After two hours, we reached it, but much of it was under water, and no way could we get a vehicle in there. So we retraced our tracks arriving back at camp about 1pm, in the drizzling rain.

A lazy afternoon in camp reading books, and cooking a salt bush mutton roast supplied by Darren and his merry men from the Waikerie butchers. A hard meal to beat.

A cosy night in the swags under the canvas.

A late start next day, getting away by 9:30am. A bit of drizzle but weather clearing. Fairly cool in the boats. Birdlife still good, and saw a large grey roo swim the river in front. A lot more wild pigs this time, and on one occasion a fox jumped out of a hollow log on the river edge and headed off into the tall grass. Camped after five, only a few kilometres from the station.

Next morning, we travelled for about half an hour before arriving at the station. Half an hour later Jim arrived with a mate in the Oka. We pulled the boats out, loaded up and back to Hay for a nice lunch put on by Beryl. A great pair of bushies from the 'old school'!

We drove down to Balranald, unloaded boats and gear at the caravan park. This boat trip was a bit more civilised than usual, because we all had a hot shower before we left.

MURRUMBIDGEE RIVER

Left at 4pm and headed downstream on a river significantly wider (50-60 metres) than our previous one. After an hour or so we made camp.

Off next morning, noticing quite a contrast between the two rivers. The Murrumbidgee Red Gums were much straighter and taller, up to 30 metres or so and far more uniform. In comparison to the *character* gums of the Lachlan.

Very few birds compared to the former, although we did see an adult White bellied Sea Eagle around mid-morning.

Soon after smoko we surprised a small grey kangaroo. It had been asleep in the sun, on the edge of the bank a metre above the water. It wasn't until we were right opposite and only four metres away, that it jumped to its feet with a startled look on its face before hopping off.

Passed a few station homesteads and fishing/hunting camps with a variety of sheds and caravans. Later in the afternoon we came across a shack with an XB Falcon ute and a Sigma station wagon that had been under water recently, write-offs. You wonder about the situation. There would have been ample warning of the flood, yet no one moved them. You see that with caravans here and on the Darling as well.

Someone saw an Echidna just before we camped. Took a bit of finding a camp high and dry, because this section of the river had the water almost up to the top of the banks, with recently flooded flats.

Next morning away at 7:30am, and cold in the boats like yesterday. The last thirty kilometres or so of the Murrumbidgee is very convoluted with plenty of hairpin bends. We saw quite a few places where water was passing back over low spots on the banks from the flats. This happens as rivers fall.

I was interested to see this section because I had been talking to Geoff Leverett who early in the year had taken his paddlewheeler (a side wheeler called the 'Bungunyah') up the Murrumbidgee to Balranald, and back. It is many years since a large boat has been up that river, and he had to use a chainsaw on a number of occasions to cut logs that were blocking him.

We reached the mouth of the Murrumbidgee at 10am and pulled up for smoko, lighting a fire to warm ourselves. Then we turned down the third river of the trip, the Mighty Murray, still flowing at nearly four kilometres an hour.

After an hour or so we came to the little settlement of Boundary Bend, seeing our first human beings since Balranald. In quick succession we passed three Chinese blokes fishing. Most of this area is state forest, and river quite remote. Passed a number of huge pumps, that were not here when I came down here on my raft seven years ago. Camped in forest.

Next day we boated through Robinvale to Euston, ending a varied boat trip on three rivers of four hundred and forty kilometres.

18 WILD RIVERS AND ANGRY RIVERS – OUR CHOICE

The decisions made in 2013 and a bit later, regarding the ongoing management of the Murray Darling Basin are vital to the future of South Eastern Australia.

It is indeed the *food bowl of Australia,* and will be required to feed and sustain a growing population into the future.

In a bit over two hundred years since European settlement in this country the Murray Darling system has been *hammered.*

The great Mallee scrubs in the southern regions have been largely cleared, increasing salinity and other land degradation. Much of the bush in the upper tributaries has also been cleared, with massive overstocking with sheep and cattle, not to mention the introduced ferals like rabbits and goats. The net result of all of this activity has totally changed the character of this great river system. Before European settlement the water would enter the system steadily, slowed down by the vegetation. As it progressed down the many creeks and tributaries it would encounter impediments and blockages such as thick vegetation and log jams, causing the water to easily spill out on to the flood plain. The silt deposited, would guarantee the ongoing health of the flood plains, which are often described as the lungs of the river. The waters would find their way back into the main channels before again spreading out. Australia is predominantly a flat country, and this is the way our rivers have always worked.

What happens now is that heavy rain rushes off mountains in many cases cleared of their native vegetation, and into the channels, cut deeper and deeper in recent times by this fast flowing water. Unless it's a *flood year* the water doesn't have a chance to spread out on the flats, so their natural fertility is no longer guaranteed.

Then came the locks. Firstly, to ensure twelve months of the year access for the paddle steamers, and then to provide regular water for the growing irrigation industry.

So, for better or worse, this is what we have. No longer a healthy wild river, but if rivers have a soul, you can bet your life they would be pretty angry by now.

In the past, you could put our mistakes down to ignorance and greed. Now though, it is mainly greed. You could say we know most of the answers. Peter Andrews, in his amazing double feature ABC '*Australian Story*' and in his two books '*Back from the Brink*' and '*Beyond the Brink*', has shown what can be done, and has gone ahead and proven it. The shameful apathy of public departments, professional snobbery and jealousy, and criticism from vested interests impacted severely on his personal life. In recent times, this man ahead of his time showed the Australian public what can be done. It's not rocket science, mostly just common sense from a man who understood how our rivers work. Fortunately he gained the backing of powerful Australians such as Gerald Harvey and ex Governor Sir Peter Jeffery.

A large number of savvy land owners are quietly implementing his ways, even though some of the practices are still *illegal*.

The only *wild river* left in the Murray Darling Basin is the Paroo. This river is more flats than channel anyway, but it does what the rest used to do. *Wobbly* legislation still prevents any damming along its length, but this is constantly being challenged, and we must be vigilant. A few years back I was lucky enough to strike the conditions that enabled me to travel much of its southern course by boat.

Most thinking people now accept the reality of global warming, so the one unknown factor (the big one) is how much water is going to come down the Murray and Darling in the coming years.

But we have to expect there will be less, and long droughts are a reality. We have only been here for two hundred years, so for all we know there may have been droughts twice as long back in the past. During this last one, water was continually sucked out, almost resulting in the loss of several species of water birds, because they simply had nowhere to go.

You get the idea that *economy* is more important than *ecology* but how wrong is that. Everywhere you look in Australia today, *short term gain* is the nature of the game. Whether it be the insidious coal seam gas industry, threatening our precious underground water and compromising some of our richest farmland. Massive revenue for cash strapped State Governments but by all accounts all gone by twenty years, leaving us with what you would shudder to think.

I live in the South Australian Riverland, and regularly see and hear prominent irrigators going on about there being too much water allocated for the environment, and not enough for irrigation. These people are usually hard working and supposedly intelligent members of our society, but I think to myself that if that is the case – don't they consider their kids, and their grandchildren, who will have to deal with the environmental mess that will be the result if we don't look after this precious asset.

I am the first to agree that there needs to be a balance for communities to remain viable, and that is very difficult to judge. But we are not necessarily dealing with an infinite resource, and that is the bottom line. Look after the goose that lays the golden eggs otherwise there will be only toast for breakfast down the track.

Then there are those other wild and *happy* rivers such as the Cooper and Diamantina. Periodically, there is pressure to grow cotton on their upper parts, and so far public pressure has prevented it. This gives me cause for optimism as many of the people that stick up for these rivers have never been near them. Although I am very wary of the internet, it is a hugely powerful tool for protection of the environment into the future.

We are all Australian, and you would reckon that if we can't work together and solve this problem, then what hope does the rest of the world have in their matters. But it doesn't necessarily look that promising. South

Australian fruit growers in particular, who are on the end of the food chain when it comes to water, are the most efficient in the country. They have had to be. Yet, when you talk to many up river state irrigators, they don't' really care about the *croweaters*. They don't give a stuff about the lower lakes or the Coorong, so long as they have enough water. The cotton growers can fill their massive dams, and then *yard up* water on the flood plains as well in many cases. That is pure selfish greed in my book.

We have to keep fighting for the legal growing of Hemp (nothing to do with the smoking of *dope*) the wonder fibre that can phase out the growing of cotton – it needs very little water and no insecticides. It is getting closer to fruition, but the powerful government lobbies still have the politicians by the *short and curlies*, and it will be a while yet.

But when it gets down to it, it is pure politics that is preventing the Murray River from regaining much of its former health. It is a regulated system and that is not going to change. However, during years of high flows, the system (the locks) can be manipulated to get water on to the flood plains periodically, which is vital for the ongoing health of the river. The reason this is not undertaken is because of the tens of millions of dollars' worth of housing (not shacks) that has been allowed (in South Australia's case) along the river between Morgan and Murray Bridge. Massive revenue for a broke Government.

The salt interception schemes, always intended as a part time solution for salinity, are a time-bomb waiting to happen. According to some local authorities, it is already happening.

Many flood plains are regulated, allowing water to come in and held, usually until it dries up causing salt build up to occur. The natural way (that can be replicated by raising and lowering the boards on the locks) allows the water to come in on a high river, and flow out when the water drops, taking most of the salt down the river as it leaves.

Unless there is one competent dedicated body free from Government interference running the Murray Darling Basin, in times of low water, State Governments will make decisions resulting in the environment being on the end of the food chain.

As is so often the case, the knowledgeable local experts (who mostly have no formal qualifications) are not consulted – or if they are, their input is used with the politicians and *boffins* getting the credit. Nothing changes.

*I am only a relative newcomer to the Murray River. Some of the contents of this chapter are from my own observations, but much of it comes from people who have lived and worked on it all of their lives.

19
THREE GOOD MEN

BILL OLIVER

Bill has passed on in outback parlance, to the other side of the sandhill, and everyone's individual beliefs will deal with that very important factor.

What we, his family and friends, have to accept is that he is no longer with us.

Bill was never what you would call a *shrinking violet*. There are those in the community that would describe him as controversial, but to me, that is not a derogative term. He was outspoken on many issues, particularly political ones. He would not tolerate fools easily and had an absolute loathing of unnecessary bureaucracy.

His *hobby horses* were many and varied, but the one that led the field, was the rights of the individual. It upset him as it does me, to see hard won rights and privileges eroded by gutless government decisions, taking the easy way out.

He didn't subscribe to the apathy of the average Australian, adopting the *she'll be right* outlook.

Bill was heavily involved in various organizations, which when it was all boiled down, stood up for the *Australian way of life,* as it used to be. This is something that should be our *Holy Grail,* and to me this is one of his important legacies.

Bill, to put it politely, had little time for banks, and there are a number of individuals in the higher echelons of that industry who wouldn't be among the mourners here today.

Various local council officials would also come into that category, particularly those who ventured uninvited onto *Whitehill Farm.* Their exit lacked the dignity of their entrance, as they fled, pierced by metaphorical arrows of well researched facts.

After several of these on ground skirmishes, the council fire power resorted to the paper artillery method of firing letters to Box 11, McLaren Vale. Many of you would know the issues in question.

He was an enthusiastic *Son of McLaren Vale* and over the years a willing contributor to the social fabric of the *Vale,* but like myself and many others that grew up here, he was unhappy with the element of dormitory suburbs status, that is a big part of McLaren Vale today. He described himself as an urban farmer.

My own association with the Oliver family goes back to when as kids I picked apricots for Bill's father, Leo – another unforgettable character who left his mark on this district.

I am 7 years older than Bill, so he and Shaye were the *Oliver kids,* full of mischief and living a good Aussie country life. It wasn't really until the 1960's that my unbroken association and mateship with Bill began. From the very early days of my safari business, Bill became a regular driver, and later on, operated some trips for me. More of that later.

A hugely important part of Bill's life was his love of and involvement in flying. I would say that one of his earliest disappointments was when, because of misdiagnosed colour blindness, he was unable to complete his commercial pilot training. This was a large blow to Bill. He nevertheless obtained his pilot licence and in recent times spent a number of fulfilling years as an ultralight instructor. He excelled at this, and I personally know a number of current flyers who would bear testimony to his skills as a patient and thorough instructor. Absent here were his often *Gung ho* and radical attitudes to other aspects of his life. A true professional.

I have flown a lot in light aircrafts in the course of my business (with other pilots) and including many hours with Bill, and have never felt safer in an aircraft. He learnt to fly a gyrocopter, and owned one. On one memorable occasion I convinced myself it was the best way to become as one with the Wedge tail Eagles and Patti and I accompanied him to an introductory training lesson at Karoonda, SA. After Bill had his go, I found myself next to the gears and works, the instructor rattling down a dirt strip, with my own *under carriage* dangerously close to the gravel.

Feeling like I was in a runaway pram, and minutes later at 150 metres, being told by the instructor that I was trying to sit on his knee. That brief experience was enough for me, but Bill went on and completed his training.

I know that several years ago when Bill was forced to give up his flying for health reasons, it was a huge blow to him, even though Bill rarely spoke about it.

In the context of Patti's and my working relationship with Bill, we have thousands of good and humorous memories.

To me his loyalty and enthusiasm I most prized. A good bush driver, competent, and good with people.

His outspokenness would sometimes *ruffle feathers*, but there are a lot of feathers around that need ruffling.

One memorable incident comes to mind. We were on the Canning Stock route with a *legal* group that we carried regularly for over 20 years. The group was led by a larger than life High Court judge. The group drank lots of grog each night, and the camp was noisy. On this occasion I had suffered a *bad day at the office*, with a rare earache. That evening, I propped myself up against my swag, attempting to get a word in edgeways, pertaining to the next day's activity, but there was no pause in the *racket*.

Suddenly Bill jumped up and yelled, "SHUT UP!" As startled and surprised faces looked at him, he followed up with "You're just a mob of educated Dickheads!" The *judge* in question (an ex spitfire pilot and top Rugby player in his youth) came close to a physical reaction, before apologising to me for their insensitive behaviour. The next day the same man and others acknowledged that Bill definitely had a point.

There are numerous others, but I am not writing a book on the subject.

His example of challenging *Sacred cows* and other negative factors endangering our beloved Australian way of life, should serve as an example to all. But Bill wouldn't just dwell on the negatives. He exulted in the positives.

All of you, who knew him well, would know his favourite exclamation and I will leave you with it, "Isn't It Amazing!!"

ADAM PLATTE

The Man from Oodnadatta

It's not hard to sing the praises of Adam Platte. I've known Adam and Lynnie for over 30 years and very much valued their friendship. Even though there have been gaps of a number of years between meetings.

Adam was *the* man from Oodnadatta, much as his former boss, Yaro Pecanek had been before him. The well-known saying "Sydney or the bush" comes to mind. Although Adam came from across the border he very soon became a fair dinkum *crow eater* after choosing Oodnadatta as his home. There was more to his trademark, pink everything than just a clever marketing ploy with the colour pink very well represented in the landscape in which he lived. Pretty well single-handedly, his perseverance, including a massive unique signage along the roads in his region meant that the Oodnadatta track became an official feature.

His signs right across the Simpson Desert being great assistance to desert travellers, until some bureaucratic buffoonery chose to remove most of them.

He was a tireless campaigner over many years for outback roads and services, and would never let up on the bureaucrats. Together he and Lynnie have helped countless travellers, and probably saved the lives of a few.

Adam was a modern day bushman who didn't suffer fools easily, but helped hundreds of people in many different ways. The most trouble anybody would have with Adam was working out how to pronounce his surname!

I had a number of things in common with Adam, in particular a love of Peugeot cars. If he was driving a Peugeot on that fateful day, he may very well still be with us. His funeral and wake was truly a huge celebration of his life, and it is significant that an old Peugeot was among one of his favourite cars *standing guard* out the front of the venue.

He was a good soldier in the war against the excesses of *Occupational Health and Safety* that is slowly bringing the country to its knees. It's a pity more people wouldn't follow his example in speaking up.

If Adam was the man from Oodnadatta, then Lynnie was the *woman from Oodnadatta*. Behind Adam all the way, and strong in her own right. Much loved by both white and aboriginal inhabitants.

Adam was an outback character. Strong and reliable with a quiet sense of humour, he was someone I was proud to know.

If there is a positive in this tragic loss, it is that he died doing something he loved – driving a rally car.

LEN JOHNSON (TWO MILE SHEEDY)

(Read at his funeral)

The last time I saw Len Johnson was when Patti and I visited him and Joyce at their place in Esperence.

He had put on a bit of weight since I'd last seen him, and his arthritis was giving him a hard time. Apart from that though, he was the same old *Two Mile Sheedy* I had always known. The thing about fair dinkum mates or friends, is that it doesn't matter how long it is between sightings – you just carry on like it was yesterday.

Anyway, after we had been there for a few hours, Joyce told Len he had to go into town and pick up some medication, so I said I would drive him in, provided I could drive his very excellent old Mercedes. We duly arrived at the doctors' waiting room, for what I expected would be a routine picking up of the pills, as it were. How wrong I was, and why should I have expected it to be *routine*, with this man! I accompanied him into the doctor's rooms, rather than waiting in the *Merc,* not sure why, but was soon to find out. *Sheedy* stood in the doorway of the waiting room, and surveyed the usual *doctors' waiting room scene.* You know what I mean – people sitting staring at the opposite wall, with hopefully a painting to focus on, no one saying a word, and everyone looking miserable. All that was about to change. "What's the matter with you bastards?" roared *Two Mile,* "You look like you've all got a dose of the shits!"

No terrorist could have wrought such havoc. It was like every one of those poor buggers had had a red hot crowbar poked up their bums! Once they had lobbed back in their seats, they stared in wide-eyed amazement as Len shuffled across the waiting room to the receptionist's desk, manned by an attractive young sheila, who, by the look on her face, had enjoyed her best moment at work for weeks or forever. That little performance was *vintage* Two Mile Sheedy, and as I stood in the doorway, a delighted onlooker, I couldn't help but notice the change that had come over the assembled. I would describe the average reaction as varying from one of nervous excitement, with a fair dose of embarrassment in a few, to a mix of pseudo outrage in a few possible *Pillars of Society,* to open delight in the rest. As Len departed the waiting room with a "see you later cobs", and we headed for the street, I could hear sounds of animated talk and laughter back in the waiting room. Whatever the patients' problems, Len had blown them away for a while, and given them something good to take home to their families.

Lennie Johnson was no angel, and depending on your beliefs, some of you could expect him to rewrite the angels' manual if/when he joins them up there. I would never have described him as *lawless,* but he had a lot of trouble tolerating *stupid* laws (like a few of us), and made an art form out of ignoring them. That's a lot easier to do when you live and work on the Nullarbor Plain, which is where I knew Len, not to forget his excellent wife Joyce. You would know the saying, "Behind every good man, is even a better or stronger woman", and never was it better applied than here. Could I be so bold as to say that there is no doubt in my mind, that if it wasn't for one of Joyce's ultimatums to Len regarding his *over enthusiastic drinking habits,* then his funeral would no doubt have been held many years earlier.

I called on Len at Googarri about six months after he had been relegated to one can of light beer a day. When he opened the door I thought I had seen a bloody ghost! He was white as a freshly washed calico bag, and had a look of uncertainty about him, and I seriously thought he was on his way out. But he wasn't – not then. Joyce knew what she was doing, and the next time I saw him, he was a much improved version of the same old *Two Mile Sheedy*, and as far as I'm concerned, has continued to be to the *final curtain*.

Len was a dreamer, ever since I had known him (early 1960's) he talked about one day owning his own sheep station – a pretty hard thing to do *on the bones of your arse* as he used to say. But he did, and he and Joyce later bought Goongarri Station, against all the odds. He was a bushman of the old school, a very hard worker, and possessed a good imagination. Goongarri was 1036 square kilometres (400 square miles) of mostly thick Mulga bush, and it was hard to make a living out of sheep. So money was made from a mix of contracting, wool, gold mining, and last but not least – selling Mulga posts to *cockies* down at Esperence who were too miserable (said kindly) to buy treated pine. Any bushman knows that most inland hardwoods rot out in twenty years or so if they are planted outside their natural area, in wetter country. But you couldn't tell them, and I'm not sure if Len tried too hard! So Len became, as far as I know, the only officially sanctioned Mulga cutter in Australia. A nice irony. Many are the stories of his *boundary riding* Kalgoorlie, avoiding the boys in blue with his sometimes dubious (over) loads of Mulga posts, heading south to Esperence.

He was the master practical joker, and if you have read my book *Mulga Madness* and a couple of my other books, because there's no time here. I was his willing apprentice in this area, and I've always been grateful for the bush skills he passed onto me. Some of them not easy to come by these days.

Now I have to finish this, and I might just tell you that I am writing on a Mulga table made of timber that Len selected and cut in 1984. It's one of my most prized possessions and contains a plaque explaining its origins. You need to read *Mulga Madness* to get the full story, but here's a little bit.

In 1984 we pulled into Goongarri to pick up three camels on the way to do a 40 day camel expedition (16 camels) across the Gibson Desert. As we left Len promised me he would have Mulga posts ready on my return. When we returned 40 odd days later and called into the station for the night, he suddenly remembered the posts! He was gone for a number of hours. As we were loading up next morning, he delivered the freshly cut posts, which were loaded with great difficulty onto the front rack of my International Blitz truck. That's the sort of mate he was.

Just before he passed away, I was talking to him. As most of you would know, he is a *croweater* – a South Australian. We were having a bit of a talk and I said something like "Len, I reckon I'll be keeping a look out for any crows behaving suspiciously, because, I reckon you are going to come back as a crow!" He chuckled a bit and replied, "No mate, I reckon I'm going to come back as a CROWBAR!" Vintage Len Johnson to the end. Travel well *Sheedy*, wherever you go!

POST SCRIPT

Now there is something that you, the family, friends and mates of Len, need to know. It concerns the levitation of Len's spirit. Not sure where it's headed, but popular belief says upward (unless you're an evil bastard. We won't go there!) Therefore in consultation with the family, I've arranged for one of Lennie's Nullarbor mates (Don Hogg) to organise a bit of transport for the said soul. Because Len is an old Croweater (South Australian), two fine Nullarbor crows have been awarded the contract to make sure Len's spirit gets aloft. These crows won't let us down, because most crows caught in Don's chook yard don't live to see another day. When you are in the know, you can definitely trust a crow. Therefore a small ceremony will take place after these formalities. These crows have a *homing* tendency and will head for the Nullarbor. Go the Crows!

PSS: Unfortunately, Don was unable to secure the services of the said crows, but the good intentions were there.

*I spent a lot of time working (and playing!) with Len Johnson since 1962, and he features in many of my books.

20 PADDLEWHEELER UP THE DARLING

Our longest river, the Darling, has a colourful history and is an icon of the Australian outback. Together with its web of tributaries it drains an enormous area, and is the main *feeder* for the Murray River.

Before paddlesteamers came on the scene in the 1860s, there were a scattering of sheep stations (mainly), but the isolation was intense. They were supplied mostly by bullock wagon with often half a year going by between supplies. When the paddlesteamer era began, the country was transformed, with regular visits. The quality of life, particularly for women, was greatly enhanced. Much has been written about this colourful period of our history.

Then irrigation arrived, and you could say that irrigation replaced navigation – by big boats anyway. A series of weirs and bridges (that didn't *open*) created a formidable barrier, and there were few locks like those on the Murray.

The last load of wool was taken out from Central Para Station in 1956 and Harry Pollard has some interesting history relating to the Darling River in the big floods of 1956. His father owned the paddlesteamer the *Success* and had a contract to bring the wool out from Para Station between Wentworth and Pooncarie. 19 year old Harry was part of the crew and was operating the barge *Dega,* towed by the *Success.* Hopefully this episode and more will be recorded in book form in the near future.

With the *wet* years of 2009-2011, the Darling, like most inland rivers was running most of the time, after being sucked nearly dry for many years with irrigation, and one of the longest droughts in European history. The massive Menindee Lakes system filled, and with good rains the country was in great heart.

I was busy operating small boat trips, mostly down the flooding Warburton and Cooper Rivers to Lake Eyre, but I did several trips in the Darling as well. The longer I spent on the Darling the more I dreamed about attempting to get my 18 metre paddlewheeler (the Dromedary) up this great river.

So in 2011 I decided to try and get up as far as Pooncarie, where the Pooncarie bridge would prevent further travel. I left home (Weston Flat on the Murray near Morgan) and a week later arrived in Wentworth. That part of the journey wasn't without incidents. Garry Duncan, Graham Radford (who lived on the Murray) and Len Cooper from Jamestown were on board with me. The first night we pulled up at a little stone hut on Graham's property near Wigley Flat. Garry lived next to him. Graham and Garry's wives (Elly and Lou) had organised a *fine feast* and we enjoyed a very good night.

Next morning Len and I got away before seven. We were putting in long days, taking it in turns on the wheel. About mid afternoon I was on the wheel, and Len said he was going back for a snooze in the hammock, at the rear of the boat. A couple of minutes later he reappeared. His usual ruddy face was white as a sheet. He said "come and have a look". I put the Dromedary in *neutral* and went with Len. He pointed to the rafters above the hammock and there was a large Murray Darling carpet python coiled above the hammock. That's when Len lost his colour!

We continued on (Len gave the hammock a miss) and I rang Graham and Garry on the mobile to tell them about the python, because it must have come on board the night before.

As I was talking *our* python came gliding past the open window of the wheelhouse, a metre from me – I nearly swallowed the phone! It went around on the iron in front of the wheel, and part coiled around the metal camel that is fixed there. Then, as we watched in total fascination, it moved to the edge of the iron, and fixing its small bare whip tail around a rivet, hung down until it was a metre off the railing, and dropped on to the rail where it coiled itself. A good trick. It then proceeded to travel around the bow of the boat, and down the starboard railing. When it passed the glass door near the cabin, Billy spotted it, and went absolutely *mental*. The snake continued on to the back of the boat. Len quickly closed all doors and windows as we wanted to keep it outside. It would either eat Billycan, or he would eat the python – neither was acceptable. It ended up coiled on top of the barbecue at the stern, and by this time it was getting dark. We placed a large empty carton with a blanket in it, hoping our visitor might camp in there. However, by the time we moored at about eight o'clock, there was no sign of our friend, and we reckon he must have dropped off. I hope he has found a satisfactory home.

With a high river most of the lock chambers were closed, and we were using the nav passes. This causes a faster flow of water, and too much for houseboats to travel through, and consequently we pretty much had the river to ourselves. We were pulled up for lunch the next day, and saw an echidna swimming by. The current was probably too fast for it to get out, and I hoped he managed it somewhere before he made Lake Alexandrina!

When we approached Lock 8, we could see the flow was really fast through the nav pass, so I steered into it with the throttle wide open. There were half a dozen people at the lock, watching with interest.

The Dromedary became slower and slower, until we were not moving forward at all, and that's when I started to age a bit.

Finally, after a minute or so (that seemed like an hour!) we began to slowly progress, and then were under way again when free of the lock. We decided that for the next lock, we would put all of our fuel down at the stern, along with anything else that had a bit of weight. It would give the paddle boards a few more centimetres under water, and should help. Andrew

Cook was now one of the lock masters at Lock 9, and was the builder of the Dromedary. That night we pulled up and camped just below the lock. Andrew met us and said he would give us a hand next morning.

In the morning, with Andrew on board, we approached the lock, and the water seemed to be as fast as Lock 8. Andrew's wife, Anne, was on the lock chamber wall taking a photograph of the boat. Then, two things happened pretty well simultaneously. We gradually lost power and began to drift backwards, but towards the lock wall. Then, we lost steering – we were pulling pretty hard on the wheel not quite understanding the power loss. As the boat came up against the railing, Andrew jumped out, and tied the boat up. Then we went and inspected the damage. The rear shaft had broken on the port side, and the steering cable had let go at a clamp. The steering didn't take long to fix, but it took three hours of Andrew on the welder to fix and reinforce the shaft. There had been a huge strain on it coming through the fast flowing nav passes.

Before leaving Lock 9 we had a look at the 'Daisy', an old paddlesteamer that Andrew was restoring. It had sunk at Menindee in 1948, and Andrew managed to salvage half a dozen of the old red gum planks. He has refitted it with seasoned Karri from WA and hopes to have it in the river later in 2013.

That night we camped at Fort Courage, a fishing camp/caravan park on the NSW side. Brenton Hicks, Graham Rivers and Ben Esop were there to come aboard for the trip up to Pooncarie.

Next morning we arrived in Wentworth, spending a few hours there while we waited for the bridge on the Darling to open up for us.

After lunch we headed on up the Darling, a lot narrower river than the one that we had left. The water for the first 30 kilometres or so is controlled by the Murray locks, but it was much higher now due to the amount of water coming down. The first 40 kilometres or so is relatively straight with a number of moderate bends, but as the irrigated fruit blocks give way to station country the real meandering begins. Many of the bends are *hairpins*, and full concentration is required. We had a nice camp, moored amongst thick river gums, having done 80 kilometres. 42 degrees today but on the water it was nice.

Next morning, under way before 6 am Bird life was improving and saw a few small flocks of budgerigars. After lunch we moored at the old wharf at Central Para Station, and had a yarn to the caretaker, Don Millard. This homestead sits right on the extreme edge of the Darling on high banks. Don showed us where a huge red gum branch had fallen on the old quarters (now tourist accommodation) where a lady had been sleeping only days earlier. Certainly her day to buy a lottery ticket!

Don, a keen photographer took several photographs from different vantage points as we moved along, and that night came up in a tinny and had a beer with us.

A full day's travel next day, the only drama being when Len (on the wheel) headed into a back water by mistake on a sharp bend. Not hard to do, with the high river covering the flats each side in many places. We actually went aground in one spot, and bent the new lugs (that Andrew had welded on the shaft) slightly, but no real damage. Took a while to gingerly reverse back out into the channel, poling as we went. All good experience.

Had a shower of rain through the night. We arrived at Minda Station after lunch, and met Philip and Sally Wakefield. We took their two young boys on board and continued onto Tarcoola Station owned by Colin and Pat Wakefield. This was where I had arranged to moor the Dromedary for 9 days before our return trip. We had a really good mooring with no large overhanging branches. Later that afternoon Colin and Philip Wakefield ran us back by vehicle to Fort Courage, where we took off for home in our various vehicles.

On February 13th, Darren Wallace, Andrew Cook, Peter Jones and I drove back to Tarcoola Station, camping on the Dromedary that night.

Next morning we got under way, and travelled the 5 kilometres or so up to the Pooncarie bridge. This is one of the lower bridges on the Darling, and there was no way we were going to get under it, as expected.

After a bit of a walk around, we executed a tricky little turn around, not easy with a sternwheeler in a narrow fast flowing river. This is one reason that the sidewheelers evolved in Australia – much easier to turn in confined spaces, compared to the wide Mississippi River in America. In this instance we started up and poled the bow out of the slack water into the current, and when it was just past right angles to the bank, gave it full throttle on a right hand lock. We swung around, missing the trees on the other bank by about 6 metres.

Back down to Tarcoola, and Colin and Pat came on board as far as Minda. We had lunch there, before heading downstream. A lot more concentration was required going with the flow particularly on the bends. Once you are committed there is no turning back, especially when saplings (some quite large) are growing in the river and you have to travel between them. This is one hazard the old paddlesteamers didn't have. These saplings grew up, mostly during the last long drought, and many of them were up to 10 metres high and quite solid. If this river had regular navigation they probably would have been removed.

An hour or so after leaving Minda, I realised I hadn't seen Billy and went for a look. He wasn't on board. We pulled in to a mooring and I began trying to contact Philip Wakefield on his mobile. After half an hour I managed to get hold of him, and asked him if he had seen a Jack Russell. He reckoned he had one sitting up on a chair in his lounge watching TV with the kids! That was a big relief – seems he had jumped off the boat to play with the station dogs as we were concentrating on leaving Minda. Some overhanging trees had made it awkward. Philip arranged to drive back across the Pooncarie bridge and back down to Lethro Station on the east bank. The road on the west side was under water. Darren and I travelled back 8 kilometres to Lethro in the Zodiak and picked the little bugger up.

When we camped that night, we found a faulty bearing on the final drive shaft. It was actually running on the steel housing of the hull. Not good, but we decided to keep going, and get to a place with better access to us.

As we approached Bertundie Station we had a concern regarding a group of very large young river gums in the river on a sharp bend. I decided to hand the wheel over to Andrew, who was vastly more experienced than I was. As we approached in the fast current, I saw a bloke on the high bank with a camera. He should do well, I thought. It was pretty scary, but Andrew handled it with skill, and we got through without any damage. We all needed a coffee after that.

We kept lubricating the crook bearing regularly. Later on I overshot a sharp bend, ending up out on the floodplain, and that afternoon Peter did the same, ending up amongst a lot of stumps and dead trees. It took about half an hour to pole out in reverse and get going again.

We were making good miles, and with the bearing seeming no worse, I decided to try and make for Baldwyn's boatyard in Mildura.

Around eleven thirty we arrived at Wentworth and moored above the Wentworth bridge. Darren and I drove back up to Tarcoola to pick up the Oka and returned to Wentworth. We went under the raised bridge early afternoon, and headed upstream for Mildura, camping below the Abbottsford bridge. We got our speed down to 5 kilometres an hour to ease the pressure on the bearing. Pretty amazing how it was still operating.

Under the Abbottsford bridge next morning through a peasouper fog, with visibility down to 50 metres. That afternoon, where the boat was to be slipped and various jobs done including the bearing fixed. We drove home that afternoon.

When the work was completed on the Dromedary, Peter Jones drove Patti and I up to Mildura, and we both travelled back home in about 5 days, with David Thamm swapping over with Patti in Renmark.

In June I did a trip down to Lake Alexandrina and back with a few mates, plus a few shorter trips through the summer.

On March 7th Andy Butler, Mike and Meredith Arnold and I left my mooring at Weston Flat, heading upstream. Camping in Waikerie that night, Mike, Andy and I continued on, heading for Wentworth.

Peter Young and Don Ranson joined us at Berri. We had to leave the boat at Lock 8 due to repairs on the lock, and on March 23rd, John Teague and Barry Peterson returned with me to the lock. We ended up spending a few days driving around the countryside as work still wasn't completed, and eventually we travelled on to Wentworth and about 30 kilometres up the Darling, returning downstream to Wentworth the following day.

The Dromedary was moored in Wentworth (a good mooring organised by John Graham) from March 30th to June 10th.

BOURKE OR BUST

On June 11th 2012 we left Wentworth with Andy Butler, John Arnold (an old riverboat man), Fred and Lyn Murray-Walker, and John and Barbara Sergeant on board (and *Billycan*). That night we camped not far from a sidewheeler called the *Bungunya*. Geoff Leverett, the owner of this boat had earlier in the year taken it up the flooding Murrumbidgee River to Balranald.

The river was a lot lower than I had expected. Water releases from the Menindee Lakes are controlled by Canberra and the fluctuating levels between Menindee and Wentworth often frustrate the locals. Barry Philp is in charge of the Menindee Lakes system at Menindee, does an excellent job, and has been very helpful to me, but can't always guarantee water depths at various times. I was expecting to have to take my wheelhouse off to get under the Pooncarie bridge, and John Arnold (an engineer) was going to be in charge of that tricky operation. We would go under and then put it back on, on the other side.

However, next morning we drove up on to some kind of a snag (probably a whole tree) and there we stayed. We could move the boat around, but no way could we get off it, and I was beginning to think we might have to establish a colony there! Finally, using a block and tackle, we were able to get off, after nearly two hours. The Dromedary had a long dent in the bottom of the hull, but no other damage.

We were due to have lunch with some friends (Colin and Robin Harrington) but we were running nearly half a day late and they had to go to Adelaide that afternoon. However, they had left us a nice bag of lemons on the bank, which meant that whatever problems we might encounter, scurvy wouldn't be one of them!

As we progressed we had to continually negotiate all sorts of snags, and the river was dropping around 3 inches (7.6 centimetres) every day. Sometimes we would travel for a couple of hours with hardly a snag, and would just begin to relax a bit before entering another snaggy section.

We were travelling steadily along one afternoon when I saw a tinny travelling ahead of us with two blokes in it. As we came closer I realised they hadn't seen us. We also noticed there was an illegal drum net in the boat. When I had approached to within 20 metres of the tinny, I gave a long blast on the horn. The blokes practically became airborne, but then a very strange thing happened. As I threw the Dromedary into neutral, they put the tinny into the bank. One of them jumped out with the drum net and scampered up the bank and put it behind a skinny little sapling. He then walked with a fair degree of embarrassment back to the tinny and hopped in. They motored over to us, and a discussion took place without any mention whatsoever of the incident! We discussed the things in general for a minute or so, before getting under way again. A really humorous situation and I reckoned those two blokes would have headed straight back to their camp for a calming ale or two.

That night we came to a nice sand bar, and lit a fire, doing a saltbush mutton roast in the camp oven.

Next morning we negotiated the trees in the river near Burtundi Station, not so bad going upstream. We talked to the station people on the bank for a couple of minutes. I was concerned that a weir 6 kilometres or so above the station might be near the surface with a falling river, but they couldn't tell me how much water was over it.

However we passed over it ok and soon after pulled up at Tulney Point Station on the western bank. I had been talking to Rachel Straun on the phone a couple of times, and she had been very helpful with information on river heights and conditions, as she takes a lot of interest in it. We all hopped off and had a bit of a walk around the homestead area, and then Rachel and her two little kids (Georgi and Harry), husband Steve and his father, Laurie came on board for a *smoko*. When we headed off Rachel and the kids stayed on board for a kilometre or so, while Steve took some photographs from his dinghy.

While we had smoko, Laurie had bought some old paddlewheeler photographs on board to show us. The Darling paddlwheeler history is still very much alive, particularly among the older generation that can remember them.

For a while we had been hearing a knocking sound down below, and John went down for a look. The portside drive chain had become a bit stretched, and at some stage we would have to take a link out of it. When we pulled up John rigged a board up under it to take up a bit of slack.

Next day we were travelling along. Andy was on the wheel and I was sitting up on the top seat above the wheelhouse, enjoying the river. We came to a very sharp bend and began to go around it. Then, the boat just kept heading toward the other bank without any sign of it coming around. I thought, "Shit, this isn't going to get any better", and scrambled down to the top deck. Next thing there was crashing and banging as we headed into the branches. Andy had slipped it into neutral just before, but the motor had stalled as he tried to get it into reverse.

The only damage was a broken window in the wheelhouse, and a couple of tears in the roof tarpaulin. Once we got sorted out, we analysed what the problem was. Andy said that as he went around the bend he suddenly lost steerage. John, our old *riverman,* recognised what had happened. On some of the real devil's elbow type bends, you get a reverse current running near the inside of the bend. If the boat is too close to the bank, and as the bow pokes out into the river, it is pushed downstream. Because your rudders are in slack water, you go straight ahead. Not a nice feeling. So, you have to take care not to be too close to the shore when negotiating the bends, but with a sternwheeler like the Dromedary and a narrow river, there is not much leeway often.

Another little drama next morning. We were only just underway, when the motor stopped, and wouldn't start. The boat began drifting back downstream out of control. The boys tried getting rope around a snag, but no luck, so I yelled out to throw the anchor over. They did so and it pulled us up midstream.

We had run out of fuel, but I found that hard to believe as we check it regularly. What actually happened was a two-way tap in the fuel line between the main and auxiliary tanks was knocked partly on, allowing the fuel in the main tank to run back to the auxiliary. It could have happened in a worse place.

Soon after a pair of wedge tailed eagles came down for a close look at us, which is always welcome. Birdlife had generally been good but not spectacular. We travelled without stopping for smoko or lunch, and arrived at Tarcoola Station about mid afternoon.

Pat Wakefield lent me her vehicle and we drove in to have a look at the Pooncarie bridge. Great news! As we thought, there was about a metre spare for us to get under without taking the wheelhouse off. I think John was looking forward to the challenge, but it wasn't going to be. Because of the low river we still had to get over the old and partly built new Pooncarie weirs.

That afternoon in Pooncarie we ran into Bill and Barb Arnold from Bindara station, downstream from Menindee. They were very interested in our operation, and offered us a good mooring at Bindara if it suited.

Next morning, with Pat Wakefield on board, we travelled on to the Pooncarie bridge. Dropped Fred and Lyn off to get photographs and movie of the Dromedary going under the bridge. Before we did so I chucked a handful of green vegetation into the pot belly heater which produced some impressive white smoke out of the stack as we passed under the bridge. A bit of poetic licence. This was the first time a large boat had been this far up the Darling for 65 years, so it needed something to mark the occasion.

We picked up the photographers, and then headed for the weirs. As we went over the old one there was very little water under us, and the boat spun around about 30 degrees, before she came back. A bit nerve wracking, but good to have it behind us. The little township of Pooncarie was only a couple of kilometres ahead.

It's interesting here to reflect on the difference this type of event would have in America compared to the Land of Oz. In the States, the fact that there hadn't been a paddlewheeler at the location for 65 years, would have guaranteed a brass band and a civic welcome with speeches, etc.

However as we came into the outskirts of Pooncarie you would be forgiven for thinking that the Neutron bomb had been dropped. Not a soul stirred. Then I saw a bloke walking away from the banks through the scrub, followed by a lame dog. And that was about it. As we pulled up at our arranged mooring, Colin and Yvonne Robinson were waiting for us. But you wouldn't want it any other way really. There was not enough water to proceed further so the Dromedary would wait here until water was available.

Once we had secured the boat, Colin and Yvonne ran us back to Colin and Robin Harrington's place (there's a lot of Colins around Pooncarie!) where our vehicles were waiting, and we drove home.

POONCARIE TO BINDARA

It was September 2nd before we arrived back in Pooncarie. Water had been released from Menindee Lakes, and we would now try to make Menindee. It was Mothers' Day, and there was a bit of a show at the Pub, where we headed for lunch. On board this time were myself, David Thamm, Don Barlow, and Graham Rivers would join us that evening. I left some wine, a 2007 Pirramimma Shiraz with a special Dromedary up the Darling label designed by Garry Duncan. The pub would auction it at a later date, and the money given to Pooncarie projects. The Johnsons at the McLaren Vale

Pirramimma Winery had supplied my *Birdsville Dry Red* when I owned the Birdsville Pub between 1974-79, so it was carrying on a nice little tradition.

This time, leaving Pooncarrie, we did have a send-off crowd of around 30 people. As we headed off I got Don to fire a couple of barrels of the 12 gauge shotgun from the top seat to help us on our way.

Pooncarie had been very good to us, all friendly and interested in the Dromedary being in town. It was moored just below Colin Robinson's house with steep banks and he was really on the ball. However, about a month ago Colin and Yvonne had to go to Melbourne suddenly to help a sick relative. Colin Wakefield (Tarcoola) was also keeping an eye on it. The powers that be in Canberra just happened to choose this time to shut the Menindee dame water off and the river dropped quickly. Two days later when Colin Wakefield came in to check the boat, it was on an angle on tight mooring ropes. Some water had entered the hull and the bilge pumps were still working – just. He got a team of blokes (they were shearing on Minda Station, just down river) and letting the ropes go, they *tommed* the boat back into the river. Tomming is a method using long flat planks and levering the boat back to a horizontal position. That was a close call, but probably no damage done.

We only travelled about 2 river kilometres that afternoon around to a mooring at the caravan park/sports area. We had to wait for Graham who was arriving that evening. He duly did, telling of a large wild pig that had nearly cleaned him up on the road. There's arguably less hazards travelling on rivers!

Next morning we were away early, but within half an hour we were suddenly among some very bad snags. I aimed the boat between two where I almost had enough room to pass. One on the portside had a nasty angle towards the boat, and as we passed, Graham grabbed it and ran the length of the deck keeping it off the windows – otherwise it definitely would have broken some and done timber damage. A dangerous thing to do, but he got away with it. We always have good men on board.

Later that morning we passed a goat hung up in the tangled roots of an old river gum. Graham and Don went back in the rubber duck to have a look. They ended up shooting it, as it was in a bad way having been there for some considerable time. Not often goats get into trouble like this, except where billygoats sometimes slip when feeding up in trees, and get hung up by their horns.

We were causing some confusion amongst the goats, as motors usually relate to motor bikes coming to muster them.

There was one hazard ahead of us – a phone line that crossed the river only a metre or so above the water. It had nearly decapitated us the year before when I was doing a tinny trip down the river from Menindee to Wentworth. Earlier this year, a kayaker had the same problem. I had been talking to Eddie Healey on Wyrama Station, and he was aware of the situation with the line. He gave me the name of the Telstra linesman in Mildura, whose area of responsibility it was, and he couldn't have been more helpful. He told me that due to good old Occupational Health and Safety (OH&S) regulations, they were not allowed to get a boat in the river and fix the bloody thing. He was one of the good old fashioned linesmen from the Telecom days, and he was obviously embarrassed by this. I told him that if he met us there, we would give him a hand using our Zodiak tender, so that was arranged. When we came to the location however, there was no cable visible, but a couple of new white posts either side of the river. We learnt later that he had used his own boat and that a couple of them had done the job. Should be more of it. It was just another example of how unrealistic OH & S regulations are seriously affecting every area of Australian life.

Much of our going was really good and free of snags. This time however we had our *secret weapon* with us. I had rung David Thamm some weeks back and asked him to rig up a sort of *snag indication device* that could be operated from a tinny. He had done so. It turned out to be a simple bent piece of reinforcing rod hung over the back of the boat with two plastic milk bottles for floats. The U of the rod hung a couple of feet under water, and would hit any snag at that depth, causing a bang and sometimes almost pulling the tinny up dead. Either David or Graham were in the tinny travelling a hundred metres or so in front of the big boat, and I would follow as near as possible the same track. It worked really well, as every now and then the tinny would hit a snag and they would tell me on the radio.

Midday we pulled up at Polia Station. The owner John Crozier showed us over his impressive stock handling complex. He ran cattle and Dorfer sheep. He and a few others, including a neighbour and the local mailman came down and had a cuppa on board the Dromedary.

Then three hours steady travelling, and close on dusk we came to the Wyarama boundary. Eddie Healey was standing on the bank with a tinny in his hand, and we invited him on board for dinner. We had an enjoyable evening, and he told us about the famous murder that occurred on Wyarama. This is all detailed in a book called *Killing Jodie.* For the first time the mozzies were really bad this night.

Underway early next morning. David had a mate (ex Burra) called Dennis Miller on Whurlie Station, and we were aiming to get there by midday. And we did. Lunch was on board with his wife Narine, a couple of station hands and two German girls who were working there. Narine brought gear as well and it was quite a spread. Half way through the meal David approached with a serious look on his face to inform me that a rear drive bearing was on its way out. Didn't improve my appetite.

Rather than risk it by going on, it was decided to do the job where we were. At least there was a nice sandy bank, and all the help that Whurlie could offer. David and Graham (both excellent mechanics) began pulling the shaft apart, while I got on the phone. Harry Pollard got straight on to a set of bearings in Mildura, and Jim Underwood (who makes a lot of my native timber furniture) offered to bring it up that day. He arrived about 5 pm, then turned around and drove back to Mildura (a round trip of 400 kilometres). I am forever grateful for good mates scattered around the countryside who are prepared to go the extra mile.

In the meantime Dave and Graham were doing a very difficult job without the ideal tools. Don had the chain stretched out on a horizontal dead gum, thoroughly lubricating and straightening out a few kinks. By midday the following day we were off again. We had noticed for a while that the chain and gear wasn't quite in line, and it was probably caused by the edges of the stern paddle wheel hitting hard against a bad snag earlier, pushing it slightly out of line.

Soon after we got going we ran into a *nest* of snags, broke half a paddle blade, and bent some side railing. We kept going all day until dusk, before camping. Reckoned we should be at Menindee, all things being equal inside two days, in time to be lifted around the weir while there was still enough water.

River dropped 5 centimetres overnight. We were away a bit after 6, as soon as we could see, and arrived at Bindara just after 9 o'clock. Bill Arnold had come down in his tinny to meet us. We moored at Bindara, causing a lot of interest among some tourists staying there. Bill and Barb Arnold run an excellent tourist operation with a variety of accommodation from rooms in the classic old rambling wooden homestead to cabins and camping.

When I heard what the water levels were upstream, I decided to stay at Bindara. It was very doubtful if we would have enough depth of water to get over Weir 32, about 20 kilometres downstream from Menindee. We stayed the night, and then the next day before heading home, Dave and I drove into Menindee.

We met John Nation who ran a number of enterprises in Menindee, including a small store. He proved to be an excellent *Menindee Man*. His wife Tassie's father was an old paddlesteamer skipper, and they were enthusiastic about our venture. John ran us around looking at various locations where it would be possible to get the boat out of the river, around the weir and back into the river again. After that we drove home.

BINDARA TO MENINDEE

December 3rd saw Len Cooper, Graham Rivers, Wendy Avery, Jocalyn Avers and I arrive at Bindara, with a new rise coming down the Darling from the Menindee Lakes. This one should get us to Menindee and around the main weir back into the river.

So far the only negative reaction to our trip was a phone call from the Menindee police advising me not to attempt to go over Weir 32 below Menindee, and an officer of the State Water Department giving me a hard time about not having a registered mooring and not having NSW registration on my boat. I told him I was only travelling through – not settling in the bloody country, although that could be a possibility if I ran out of water altogether. The police were only doing their job, but locals couldn't believe the attitude of the bloke from the Department. Just goes to show that *the bureaucracy* don't like the citizens *pushing the envelope* or getting *ideas above their stations*. A sad thing.

Had a good open river with minimal snags, with Len and Graham taking it in turns operating the S.I.D. (Snag Identification Device) from the tinny.

At one stage we saw 10 emus swim the river in front of the boat, and climb up an unusually easy part of the bank, leading us to wonder if this might have been a regular crossing place. I have never seen that many emus in the river at one time. Unfortunately they were nearly half a kilometre in front of us and it wasn't possible to photograph them.

Soon after on a real *devil's elbow* bend I was a bit too close in shore and a reverse current caused me to head straight across the river into timber on the other side. I was able to slow the boat before we were into the trees, and no damage was done. It was a farily narrow river there and I didn't really have much option but to be close to the bank when I went around.

55 kilometres for the day and camped near the biggest river red gum that I have seen on the Darling. Upstream from Wanda Station on the east side of the river. The river gums are a constant source of interest, and the tag of *Nature's boarding house* certainly fitted this one. It provided great biodiversity, and I identified 22 bird species in and around this tree while camped here, from Tree Martins to Boobook Owls.

Left about 7 with only 20 kilometres to go before Weir 32. Len lost steerage with more reverse current on a bend, and we had to extricate ourselves from a *Kelly's woodyard* type situation, but no harm done.

Mid morning we arrived at a predetermined location near the weir, and I phoned John Nation and Barry Philp. Barry drove down from the town and John came down in his powerboat. Then we had a look at the weir. It was the fastest flow of water I had seen yet on either the Murray or the Darling, and I was relieved that John was going to give me a tow through it. A few hundred metres before that however, was another *hazard* called *A bend*. This was a right angle bend in the river with a large dead tree in the river on the left hand side, and a broken off heavy limb sticking out on the right side, with not a very large gap in between. If John hadn't been there with his boat, I would have let the Dromedary drift into the dead tree trunk (that disappeared under water) and then tack around the bend. Would have been tricky, particularly with a fast flow coming off the weir. Anyway we hooked a line on to John's boat and away we went. Passed through *A bend* without wiping the top deck off and proceeded toward Weir 33.

The girls had gone up there with Barry to get some photographs. With the power of both boats we were slowed to about 2 kilometres an hour, but got through and moored upstream a bit for lunch. Good to have these two hazards behind us.

We arrived at the Menindee outskirts at two thirty, with a number of people here and there on the banks having a look. There was one bloke sitting in a wheelchair on a fairly high bank, fishing. I gave him a wave, but he sat as though carved in stone. Maybe he didn't believe his eyes. Anyway, hope we improved his day.

The Menindee bridge appeared ahead, and we went under with a metre to spare. I noticed a bloke in a ute drove across and then disappear out of sight. Next thing, he came racing back very fast in reverse and stopped for a look. You couldn't do that on the Sydney Harbour Bridge!

We pulled up at John Nation's mooring, with an indignant Willy Wagtail sitting on its nest a metre above the bow of the boat.

There were 20 or so people there, and Sheree from the ABC come aboard and did an interview. Bill and Barb Arnold bought the Oka in from Bindara as well as Wendy's car. This was the same place that the PS Renmark moored in 1942, the last boat to be in Menindee.

Unfortunately Canberra had pulled the plug early on the water and there was not enough to get the Dromedary back into the river above the main weir. So looked like the boat was going to be spending some time in Menindee.

Next day we moved down to a vehicle access where the local septic bloke was going to pump out our tank. However he didn't have the necessary couplings. Bill Arnold said "I'll go and make one", and headed off for Bindara saying he would meet us at the same place next day. No doubt about that man.

We headed off the 20 kilometres or so to the Menindee Weir, and camped there that night. On the way back I noticed a really good mooring, below the Railway bridge (which we had passed under the day before). I waved to a bloke near his house.

We went back and the septic bloke and Bill were at the pump out spot to meet us. Bill had knocked up a fitting on his lathe, and presented me with our own pump out hose. It worked brilliantly.

I mentioned to John Nation about the proposed mooring and he said he knew who owned the property. He reckoned that if the *blockie* was agreeable, the boat would be as safe as a house.

John told me a good story about the *blockie*. He grew apricots as near to organic as possible, when surrounded by a lot of other horticulture. He heard that his neighbour was going to spray his trees the next day which would have meant a lot of drift onto his trees.

He asked his neighbour if he wouldn't spray on that day but his neighbour said he intended to. So next morning the blockie in question climbed up on his tank stand which looked out over his neighbour's place. He had a rifle with him.

He sat up there and when the neighbour came out to set his spray unit up, he pointed his rifle at him. The neighbour changed his mind and didn't spray that day!

When we drove down to this blockie there was an interesting sign on his well-built gate. It said "Unauthorised persons, relatives and stray cats and dogs exterminated". This sounded like a very safe place to moor the Dromedary.

So we went and saw the *blockie*, and he was very happy for the boat to be moored there. We returned an hour later with the boat, and unloaded and secured it. Just before we left, the *blockie* walked out with a book in his hand, and asked if I would like to borrow it. I couldn't believe my eyes. It was *Dreadnought of the Darling* by the famous World War I war correspondent, CW Bean. A rare book. He had picked it up in a second hand book shop for a couple of dollars when he was working in the Pilbara. I said I wouldn't borrow it, but later on I was going to try and buy it from him. I said it would have a good home on the Dromedary, so we'll see what happens.

As I finish this chapter it is February 22nd 2013, and there is a fair size flood coming down the Darling. With a bit of luck I will be on my way up the Darling above Menindee, heading for Wilcannia in April. If there is not enough to get there this time, I will moor it at Nelia Gari Station. This is also a very good tourist operation owned by Greg and Lily Martin, and I would be able to do a few trips between there and the Menindee weir, as the water backs up that far from the weir when the lakes are holding good water.

My ultimate goal is to reach Bourke, before trucking the Dromedary back to the Murray. But it doesn't really matter because the journey is always better than the destination.

OTHER BOOKS BY REX ELLIS

Bush Safari

Mulga Madness

Outback by Camel

Ten Thousand Campfires

Boats in the Desert

Go with the Flow

Country Town Boy

Mopokes and Mirages

Walking with Dingoes

by Owen Davies

Coming Soon

Extraordinary accounts of Outback Expeditions, walking with Pack Goats and his own Dingoes

MAPS

Rex Ellis' *Map of the Australian Deserts*

ABOUT THE AUTHOR

Rex Ellis was born in 1942, and lives with his wife Patti in Mallee scrub on colourful cliffs, overlooking the Murray River, in South Australia. From this semi-desert base he operates his outback safari business with camels, 4WD vehicles, and boats on the desert rivers. After jackerooing and overseeing on sheep stations for 6 years, he began his safari business in 1965. In 1971, he led the first party of tourists across the Simpson Desert. Subsequent trips have been to other deserts and tropical regions, such as Cape York Peninsula, The Gulf country, and The Kimberley region. His regular 4WD trips were to The Nullarbor/Great Victoria Desert, Birdsville/Strzelecki Tracks, and Flinders Ranges. He purchased the Birdsville Pub in 1973, and for six years, used it as a base for trips into the Simpson Desert. Inland boat safaris became a speciality, after Rex made the first and only crossing of Lake Eyre by boat during the 1974 floods. Since then he has followed most of the inland's flooding rivers. In 1976 he pioneered long-haul desert camel expeditions, and has crossed all the Australian deserts. When not travelling or writing, he plants native trees, and pursues his interest in wildlife, in particular, birds. He operates his paddle wheeler, *The Dromedary,* on the Murray and Darling Rivers.

Books by **Rex Ellis**

$28.00

$19.99

$28.00

$29.99

$29.99

$28.00

$25.00

$29.99

$29.99 (novel)

$15.00

$29.99